DEPARTMENT OF THE ARMY HISTORICAL SUMMARY

DEPARTMENT
OF THE
ARMY HISTORICAL SUMMARY

FISCAL YEAR 1970

COMPILED AND EDITED

BY

WILLIAM GARDNER BELL

GOVERNMENT REPRINTS PRESS
Washington, D.C.

Printed in The United States of America
Ross & Perry, Inc. Publishers
216 G St., N.E.,
Washington, D.C. 20002
Telephone (202) 675-8300
Facsimile (801)459-7535
info@RossPerry.com

SAN 253-8555

Government Reprints Press Edition 2002

Government Reprints Press is an Imprint of Ross & Perry, Inc.

Library of Congress Control Number: 2001096862
http://www.GPOreprints.com

ISBN 1-931839-36-0

Book Cover designed by Sapna. sapna@rossperry.com

⊛ The paper used in this publication meets the requirements for permanence established by the American National Standard for Information Sciences "Permanence of Paper for Printed Library Materials" (ANSI Z39.48-1984).

Foreword

This fiscal year 1970 summary of Army expenditures, work, and accomplishments is the second annual edition to be published separately by the Army following cancellation in May 1972 of the Annual Report of the Department of Defense—a document which for two decades had incorporated the annual reports of all of the service secretaries. Continuation of the Army report sustains a document published annually since 1822, one whose earlier editions dating from 1792 were brought into print in 1832 in the military affairs volumes of *American State Papers.*

Those seeking the broad context of the military establishment that was formerly available in the consolidated Annual Report of the Department of Defense are referred to the annual posture statements of the Secretary of Defense. As those reports deal with future requirements rather than past accomplishments, annual editions of the Department of the Army Historical Summary should be consulted for the details of expenditures, work, and accomplishments that pertain to the Army.

Washington, D.C.
15 January 1973

JAMES L. COLLINS, JR.
Brigadier General, USA
Chief of Military History

Contents

DEPARTMENT OF THE ARMY HISTORICAL SUMMARY

Fiscal Year 1970

I. Introduction

Although the Vietnam War continued to be a major concern both nationally and militarily during the last year, there was a marked change of direction in the conflict that was promising for the United States and for American armed forces. Following the steady expansion in military strength and combat commitment that occurred between 1965 and 1968, and the general stabilization that took place in 1969, a significant contraction was begun in fiscal year 1970. There were reductions in over-all Army strength, division force structure, troop deployment, combat operations, and battle casualties.

Army strength at the end of June 1970 was 1,322,548—down more than 248,000 from the peak of 1,570,000 reached in June 1968. The over-all reduction was made possible by the withdrawal of about 115,000 American troops from Vietnam, almost 59,000 of them Army. This left a little over 300,000 Army troops in the combat zone in June 1970, as compared with the high of 361,000 in June 1969.

Withdrawn from Vietnam in two increments were the entire 1st Infantry Division, two brigades of the 9th Infantry Division, the 3d Brigade of the 4th Infantry Division, and the 3d Brigade of the 82d Airborne Division. The reduction, the equivalent of 2⅓ divisions, left six division forces in Vietnam. Inactivations and demobilizations, notably of the 24th Infantry Division, reduced the active Army's division force structure from 19⅔ to 17⅓ division force equivalents by year's end.

Initial withdrawals were justified by the course of events. For the most part, American, Republic of Vietnam, and Free World Military Assistance forces held the initiative throughout South Vietnam following a long period of search and destroy operations that inflicted progressively heavier losses on the Viet Cong and the North Vietnamese. Infiltration routes were regularly interdicted. The enemy's logistic base was uncovered site by site, and large stores of food, equipment, and arms were captured or destroyed. Pacification activities were expanded concurrently, weakening the enemy's hold on the populace and strengthening the Saigon government's popular support. Moreover, major operations against enemy sanctuaries in neighboring Cambodia in May and June 1970 seriously affected the enemy's ability to carry out operations in South Vietnam.

Vietnamization of the war became a central theme of American policy and the focus of American effort during the year. As the major task of equipping and training Republic of Vietnam units progressed, indigenous forces began to assume a more prominent combat role while U.S. forces turned their attention increasingly to consolidation and eventual disengagement.

The acceleration of troop deployment to Southeast Asia from the summer of 1965 to the summer of 1969 and the broadening of the fighting had produced a steady increase in U.S. casualties; monthly tolls, for example, ran as high as 1,363 soldiers killed in February and 8,298 wounded in March of 1968. Army losses were the greatest among the services.

By fiscal year 1970, on the other hand, the enemy had been severely punished, the level of combat had dropped, a troop withdrawal was in progress, and Republic of Vietnam forces were assuming increasing battlefield responsibility. Despite the operations in Cambodia, American casualties dropped sharply. Weekly losses for all services fell to three-year lows, and for the first time American casualties were less than those sustained by the Republic of Vietnam. By June 30, 1970, the United States had lost 43,000 soldiers killed over the full course of the war, including eight general officers; another 285,000 had been wounded in action, about half of whom required hospital care. The Army's total war casualties were 28,011 soldiers killed and 183,760 wounded in the 9½ years of American military involvement.

In addition to the requirements of the war, the Army continued to provide major forces in other areas of the world as a part of American contributions to collective security: 2 divisions remained in Korea and 4⅓ in Europe. Special mission forces continued on station in Berlin, the Canal Zone, Hawaii, Alaska, and Okinawa; remaining active Army division forces, augmented by Reserve Component units, formed a part of the Strategic Reserve in the continental United States.

Although the gradual stabilization of conditions in Vietnam and the withdrawal of some troops eased personnel imbalances, especially with regard to junior leaders and specialists, manpower problems were inherent in the two-year service obligation of inductees and the short tour replacement requirements for Vietnam and Korea. These strictures probably will continue until a substantial leveling-down is possible in Vietnam, bringing short tour needs into general balance with the long tour rotation base. Meanwhile, requirements will be met by a combination of individual assignment extensions, short term service curtailments, voluntary extensions and involuntary repetitive tours in Vietnam, and accelerated promotion at junior officer and noncommissioned officer levels.

The Army requested $30 billion in new funds for fiscal year 1970 operations. Following reviews by the Office of the Secretary of Defense and the Bureau of the Budget, the President requested just under $26 billion. The Congress appropriated something less than $22.5 billion. The downward turn in Vietnam and the urgency of domestic needs required the Army to meet its responsibilities with diminishing resources. Smaller appropriations and inflation placed a premium on the management of resources.

A general climate of social unrest in the nation, exacerbated in part by domestic ills and in part by an unpopular war, continued to be reflected in and to have implications for the armed forces in fiscal year 1970. Problems were both internal and external, and covered a wide range of dissent. Externally they were manifested by opposition to the draft, evasion of military service, interference with recruiting, and destruction of campus ROTC buildings; internally they took form in underground activities, racial antagonism, resistance to authority, and desertion.

Irresponsible forms of dissent were limited to relatively small numbers of citizens and soldiers. The majority of Americans, no matter what their personal feelings concerning the war or social justice, were prepared to carry out their responsibilities of citizenship and service and to work within the system and through established methods and procedures to further their views. Mindful of the basic requirements to provide a disciplined and effective force for national security, the Army reacted to responsible dissent by making certain adjustments in policies, procedures, and regulations.

Despite a rigid code of ethics, the Army is a product of the society from which it springs and has its share of human weaknesses and failings both on and off the battlefield. Several misdeeds of recent times were of some magnitude, received major publicity, and required a substantial investigative effort during the last year. Notable among them were charges of battlefield misconduct in the Son My (My Lai) area in South Vietnam and mismanagement of service clubs in various locations. Unfortunate as these incidents were, they involved only a few individuals and did not derogate the fine performance of the vast majority of American soldiers on the battlefield, at home, and elsewhere around the world.

The Army's task in the seventh decade of the twentieth century was no different from what it has been since its inception—to provide the land element of the military forces that insure U.S. national security. Some of the details of how this task was accomplished in fiscal year 1970 are covered in the following pages.

II. Operational Forces

Several factors influenced the Army's over-all operational situation during fiscal year 1970. The general reduction in the level of fighting in Vietnam, combined with initial troop withdrawals and a presidential directive to reduce oversea forces by 10 percent, led in turn to reductions in Army strength and units. Refinements and adjustments in organization, personnel and skill distribution, and logistical posture improved over-all Army readiness.

The Pacific and the Far East [1]

Early in the fiscal year, on July 9, 1969, President Richard M. Nixon ordered the 10 percent reduction in American forces overseas, based on authorized strengths as of June 30, 1969. Certain direct-hire civilians were included. The purposes were to reduce expenditures, favorably influence the balance of payments, and reduce the American presence overseas. Military forces in Vietnam and Korea and others supporting the war were exempted from the reduction. The total number of Army positions deleted in the Pacific area exceeded 2,000.

The initiation of redeployments of U.S. forces from Vietnam served as a basis for major organizational and dispositional changes that occurred in the period. U.S. forces were removed from the Mekong Delta region, and the conduct of the war there passed to the Republic of Vietnam. Redeployment of a major part of U.S. Marine Corps forces in the I Corps Tactical Zone resulted in the transfer of command responsibility for U.S. forces there to Headquarters, XXIV U.S. Army Corps. The headquarters of the 1st Logistical Command was consolidated with Headquarters, U.S. Army, Vietnam. The 10 percent reduction in the Pacific was carried out concurrently, and a major refinement of Army logistical activity was begun to bring logistical forces into line with the structure that is anticipated for the region over the next several years.

Other developments had a bearing on the Vietnam War and on the American presence and U.S. Army deployment in Southeast

---

[1] See chapter 3 for details on the Vietnam War.

Asia. The North Vietnamese in March 1970 drove Royal Lao forces from the Plain of Jars in northern Laos and threatened to overrun the Meo heartland. That offensive was conducted by regular North Vietnamese units in flagrant violation of the Geneva Accords concerning the neutrality of Laos. Following the ouster of Prince Sihanouk as Cambodia's head of state, Viet Cong and North Vietnamese forces moved out of their sanctuaries along the Cambodia-Vietnam border to spread their control over eastern Cambodia. In conjunction with their thrusts into Cambodia, the Communist forces seized two provincial capitals in southern Laos, thus securing a water supply route through Laos to compensate for their loss of the use of the Cambodian seaports of Kampot and Kampong Som (Sihanoukville). The year thus produced the first open confrontation between North Vietnamese and Cambodian forces, and for the first time since 1962 the North Vietnamese attacked Royal Laotian forces without the facade of the Pathet Lao.

In Thailand, U.S. Army authorized troop strength was reduced by about 2,900 in line with the President's 10 percent cutback. Army units continued to provide logistical support for all U.S. forces in the country. Highway construction linking northeastern Thailand with Bangkok and the port of Sattahip neared completion.

The Royal Thai Army Volunteer Force in Vietnam, for which the U.S. Army supplied training and support, completed its first full rotation of personnel from the war zone. Responsibility for operating the Thai Overseas Replacement Training Center at Kanchanaburi, Thailand, was taken over by the Royal Thai Army, as the number of U.S. advisers training Thai replacements was reduced to a small detachment. The construction of the camp was completed, and it was turned over to Thailand.

In Korea the Communist threat remained generally unchanged as North Korean pressure on the Republic of Korea in the south continued. Although the attitude of the North Koreans was more hostile than at any time since the armistice agreement was signed in 1953, there was a sharp drop in the number of incidents in the closing quarter of the year, possibly because of effective countermeasures by U.S. and Republic of Korea forces and the fact that the North Koreans have been unable to establish a viable guerrilla base among the South Koreans.

U.S. combat forces remained deployed in Korea and joined indigenous forces in the defense of the Republic of Korea. Eighth U.S. Army elements were deployed along the demilitarized zone; the I Corps (Group) defended the western avenues of approach into South Korea, with the 2d Infantry Division deployed and the 7th Infantry Division in reserve. Supporting units included the 4th Missile Command and the 38th Artillery Brigade (Air Defense), and the U.S. Military Advisory Group helped the Republic of Korea's Army of over half a million men to develop and maintain its forces.

Elsewhere in the Far East–Pacific region, U.S. Army deployment in Japan, Okinawa, and the Philippines remained generally stable. On Okinawa, in addition to Headquarters, U.S. Army, Ryukyu Islands, and Headquarters, IX Corps, the principal forces were the 2d Logistical Command, the 30th Artillery Brigade (Air Defense), the 7th Psychological Operations Group, the 1st Special Forces Group, and the 1st Civil Affairs Battalion. In Japan, the U.S. Army headquarters at Camp Zama continued to supply logistical support to U.S. and allied forces in the Far East, including military assistance, depot operations, procurement, and hospital facilities. And in the Philippines and on Taiwan, advisory groups continued to assist host countries to develop and maintain their forces.

By the end of fiscal year 1970, operational forces in the Pacific and Southeast Asia totaled seven divisions, twenty additional combat units of brigade size, five corps or equivalent headquarters, and a multitude of support elements including missile, air defense, engineer, military police, signal, and aviation units.

Europe

In Europe the United States continued to maintain an armored-mechanized and nuclear-supported force as a part of the North Atlantic Treaty Organization's land defenses in central Europe. Major forces consisted of 2 armored divisions, $2\frac{1}{3}$ mechanized infantry divisions, and 2 armored cavalry regiments. Supporting units included artillery units with a nuclear capability.

Organizational changes to streamline the command, control, and logistical organization of Army forces in Europe were completed during the year. A U.S. theater Army support command and two corps support commands were activated; a single inventory control center for the theater was established; and the U.S. Army tactical control echelon under NATO was revised.

A United Kingdom–Belgium–Netherlands–Luxemburg line of communication and port plan was also developed and approved. When implemented it will provide U.S. Army, Europe, with the units and equipment to establish a wartime line of communications through the Low Countries and to replace the line through France, whose territory was withdrawn from NATO use in 1966. The peacetime line of communications through Bremerhaven, Germany, is not suitable for wartime use.

The Army continued to participate in negotiations with the Spanish government for U.S. base rights in Spain beyond the two-year extension granted in 1969. Under existing arrangements the United States has supplied Spain with small amounts of arms and equipment and with Army advisory training assistance in their use.

Alaska and Latin America

U.S. Army, Alaska, the Army component of the Alaskan Command, continued to be responsible for the ground defense of Alaska. The tactical units were reorganized during fiscal year 1970 to make them more compatible with their missions and the Alaskan environment. The two mechanized infantry brigades were converted to light infantry: the 171st located north of the Alaskan Range at Fort Wainwright near Fairbanks, and the 172d south of the range at Fort Richardson near Anchorage. Each brigade had two maneuver battalions and a battalion of artillery; they were well suited to meet operational conditions in Alaska.

The reduction in tracked vehicles will be offset by the addition of helicopters to improve mobility. The change was prompted by the fact that maintenance of tracked vehicles is difficult under extreme winter conditions and mobility is limited across the muskeg terrain in summer. A modest but adequate mechanized capability remains in two armored cavalry troops, and an antiarmor capability is provided by the Sheridan armored reconnaissance vehicle with the Shillelagh missile.

In the Panama Canal Zone, the U.S. Army, Southern Command, maintained a force consisting of the 193d Infantry Brigade (with two infantry battalions and a mechanized battalion) and a Special Forces Group. The latter was prepared to provide mobile training teams to Latin America on request. In December 1969 the command's aviation was consolidated into the newly activated 206th Aviation Company to provide tactical mobility for the defensive forces. In March 1970 the two 40-mm. self-propelled air defense artillery batteries of the 517th Artillery were inactivated.

The Eleventh Annual Pan American Rifle Matches were held in February 1970 in the Canal Zone under the command's sponsorship. A week of small arms marksmanship and maintenance training was followed by a week of practical exercises in the form of competition between teams of the fourteen participating nations.

Army Readiness

The status of major Army units improved generally in personnel and logistics during fiscal year 1970, while their training status remained essentially unchanged. Support units remained about the same as the previous year; many units reported unsatisfactory readiness status. The orderly reduction of Army manpower during the first half of the fiscal year, through redeployments from Vietnam and subsequent unit inactivations, permitted some improvement in readiness of personnel. But toward the end of the year, reduced draft calls, failures in meeting draft calls, and changes in planned Vietnam redeployment increased the shortage of trained strength and reduced the number of personnel available for assignment to units. The result was an erosion of some of the gains in personnel readiness made earlier in the year.

Unit personnel turnover decreased in most units in the first half of the fiscal year because of higher operating strengths and fewer losses of personnel to short tour assignment. Toward the end of the year, however, turnover again approached the rates of late fiscal year 1969, the result of greater losses of personnel to short tour assignment and increased losses of draftees completing service two years after a peak induction period. Personnel turnover has been the principal limiting factor to any significant improvement in unit training readiness. The net effect of the continuous personnel rotation is to keep units from achieving a fully trained status at any given time and to force them to recycle training at the lower levels to insure basic proficiency in the primary mission.

Units operating under standard tables of organization and equipment were used to augment manpower resources available to carry out installation functions. So far as possible, tasks were assigned that were related to the missions of these units and would enhance their readiness. Unit integrity was maintained where possible. As the year closed, a study was under way to develop stationing patterns for active Army units of the baseline force that would make optimum use of their installation support capabilities.

In U.S. Army, Europe, a readiness improvement program begun in December 1968 had by June 30, 1970, brought 95 percent of reporting units up to their readiness goals for equipment on hand and placed war reserve and prepositioned stocks in a favorable condition. The improvement was achieved by shipment of equipment and supply stocks from the continental United States and redistribution of theater reserve stocks. Over $187 million in equipment was delivered during the year to achieve the improved readiness posture.

The capability to deploy rapidly and to sustain operational forces anywhere in the world is an essential ingredient of strategic planning. Rapid response is based upon force readiness in combination with airlift, sealift, and prepositioned materiel.

During the past year the rapid response capability was enhanced by the introduction of the first C–5A heavy logistic transport. Army field testing of this aircraft will continue into the coming fiscal year. With respect to prepositioned equipment, although the serviceability of unit sets of equipment continued to be less than desired, improvements were made in Europe in the area of controlled humidity storage facilities.

Of some concern is a continuing decline in the capability of the Military Sea Transportation Service (renamed Military Sealift Command) and the commercial sealift fleet to support the rapid deployment of U.S. forces during the early days of a contingency. The MSTS fleet, consisting of World War II ships, is rapidly shrinking in size, and the commercial fleet is being reduced in total size and in the number of ships suited for the deployment of Army equipment. In light of these conditions, the Army strongly supports a Navy proposal to build and charter ten multipurpose cargo ships. These ships have been specifically designed to transport military equipment; each would be able to carry over 500 vehicles in addition to helicopters and other equipment.

Army Operations Center and System

The Army Operations Center has served as the Army's primary command center during several international and domestic emergencies since its move into new and expanded facilities in the basement of the Pentagon in June 1969. The improved command and control capability afforded by the new facility and equipment assisted the Secretary of the Army and the Chief of Staff in carrying out the Army's mission. The emergency employment of Army resources during Hurricane Camille and the postal strike was controlled from the center, and it has been used by the Army Staff for several special projects.

Evolutionary improvements were made in the operations center system during the year. A new deployment reporting system became operational to evaluate the time-phased force requirements of all operational plans. This system gives the Army a means of adapting automated data processing techniques to its total and partial mobilization requirements. Plans for the next generation system for the Army Operations Center and for Army emergency relocation sites were developed during the year.

The operations center continued to co-ordinate the Army's contribution to the U.S. Secret Service in its role of protecting the President and Vice President of the United States. This support included explosive ordnance disposal personnel, helicopters, and other assorted equipment and personnel resources. In this connection, the Army received an increased number of requests from other federal agencies and civil authorities for explosive disposal assistance, involving bomb scares, disarming explosive devices, checking and disposing of war souvenirs, and providing help in transportation accidents involving explosives. Over 4,800 requests were acted upon in fiscal year 1970, compared with 3,762 in the previous year.

Civil Disturbance and Emergency Operations

Because of their organization, discipline, equipment, and geographical distribution, federal military forces are available on call to provide prompt assistance in all kinds of emergencies. In the past year Army troops were called upon to assist civil authorities on several occasions of domestic disturbance and to provide aid during a period of major natural disaster.

Requirements for federal forces to help local and state authorities restore law and order during civil disturbances were restudied during the year in the light of an apparent lessening of the threat of large-scale disorders and the increased capabilities of local and state forces resulting from improved planning, training, and equipment. As a result, the number of metropolitan areas considered likely to experience disorders of a magnitude to require federal assistance was substantially reduced, and a corresponding reduction was made in the number of active Army and U.S. Army Reserve units required to be trained and to maintain continuous readiness for civil disturbance operations.

As a precaution against the possibility of civil disturbances growing out of antiwar demonstrations, federal forces were strategically deployed on four occasions in fiscal year 1970. The first grew out of an announced demonstration against the Vietnam War scheduled for October 12, 1969. Various antiwar organizations throughout the United States pledged their support and stated their intentions to disrupt activities at several military installations. To protect installations faced with the greatest potential threat of disorder, small contingents of military forces were deployed to Fort Dix, New Jersey; Rock Island Arsenal, Illinois; Carlisle Barracks,

Pennsylvania; Boston Army Base, Massachusetts; and Fort Hamilton, New York. Disorder occurred only at Fort Dix, and it was quickly contained by local and military police.

Extensive antiwar activities occurred at Washington, D.C., in the period November 13–15, 1969. Estimates of participation ranged up to a quarter of a million people. To protect extensive federal properties and functions within the city, and to make it possible for military forces to respond quickly to requests from civil authorities for assistance, elements were positioned at key locations around Washington. The units were carefully controlled and their mission was strictly defined. As it turned out, they did not have to be used.

At New Haven, Connecticut, in the first three days of May 1970, Yale University students boycotted classes and demonstrated on the eve of the murder trial of several members of the Black Panther group, raising the prospect of violence. The governor of Connecticut requested that federal forces be positioned near the scene, and two brigades were airlifted to military installations in the area. Again their use was not required.

And finally, when antiwar organizations reacted to American military operations against enemy sanctuaries in Cambodia by announcing plans for a mass demonstration in Washington, D.C., on May 9, 1970, federal forces were once again positioned to protect citizens and federal property and functions should the need arise. An important aspect of the operation was the medical and other health-related military support made available to citizens. The occasion demonstrated the principles that guide federal military assistance to civil law enforcement agencies: federal forces respond to requests from civil authorities; they assist civil authorities to maintain law and order; only the minimum amount of force is used consistent with the situation; federal forces protect the rights and property of citizens.

In response to seventy-six requests, riot control materiel—protective masks, CS grenades, protective vests, communications equipment—was loaned to civil law enforcement agencies and the National Guard in eighteen states and the District of Columbia.

The Army has been called upon many times throughout U.S. history to perform various functions connected with labor disputes, and the duties have ranged from peacekeeping to providing essential services. During late March and early April 1970 another occasion arose in connection with a work stoppage by postal employees, and the President of the United States called upon the military services to assist the Post Office Department in maintaining essential postal services. The postal strike began on March 18 in New York City and spread rapidly to widely scattered cities. The peak of the work stoppage was reached on March 23 and 24. Mail service in thirteen states was disrupted as some 200,000 of the 750,000 postal workers were off the job.

On March 23, President Nixon declared a national emergency and directed the Secretary of Defense to respond to requests of the Postmaster General for help in restoring and maintaining postal services. The Secretary of Defense in turn designated the Secretary of the Army as executive agent. The joint operation was nicknamed Operation Graphic Hand.

Although planning for military augmentation of postal facilities had to consider the possibility of a nationwide postal strike and operational requirements in thirty-five priority cities, Graphic Hand was executed in New York City only, during the period from March 23 to April 4. The multiservice force, named Task Force New York, was under the operational control of Major General Walter M. Higgins, the commander of Fort Hamilton, New York. Over 18,500 military personnel were assigned to seventeen post offices on March 25, the peak day of operation; 12,764 were Army (750 regular Army, 6,839 National Guard, and 5,175 Army Reserve). The balance were Air National Guard and Navy, Air Force, and Marine Corps Reserve forces.

The military personnel, working under postal supervisors, sorted mail, transported it to substations and other areas, and delivered bulk mail to businesses and charitable organizations. No residential deliveries were made. According to postal officials, service personnel processed 12.8 million pieces of outgoing letter mail leaving New York City; processed 4.4 million pieces of letter mail for delivery in New York City and cased over 3.2 million pieces of mail for city delivery; delivered nearly 2 million pieces to business firms and charitable organizations; delivered 3.2 million pieces to callers; delivered 11,986 registered letters; and loaded or unloaded 96 trailers of mail.

Postal workers began returning to work on March 25, as prospects of an acceptable settlement of their wage and other grievances increased. On March 26 postal authorities canceled requirements for military augmentation of the post offices, demobilization began, and the operation was completed on April 4, 1970.

Earlier on the domestic scene, the Army Operations Center coordinated and monitored the military assistance given to civil authorities and the citizenry after Hurricane Camille struck the gulf coast with devastating force in August 1969 and moved across the southeastern United States to cause flash flooding in Virginia's James River Valley. The military services provided thousands of workers and hundreds of items of equipment and transported thousands of tons of supplies to assist disaster victims in a three-state area. Army units opened hundreds of miles of road, cleared tons of debris, provided communities with food and water, and coordinated with the Air Force the evacuation of hospital patients.

Civil Affairs and Civic Action

The major civil affairs and civic action commitments and responsibilities in oversea areas remained in Southeast Asia in 1970. Army civil affairs units in Panama, Okinawa, and the Republic of Vietnam participated in a wide variety of advisory and operational activities designed to improve agriculture, education, roads and utilities systems, and facilities, as well as in numerous other activities to encourage host-country counterpart military forces to engage in enterprises to promote the welfare of their people.

As the result of a formal resolution passed by the Congress of Micronesia, the Army joined in a unique civic action program sponsored by the Department of the Interior. A civic action team was deployed to Majuro Atoll in the Marshall Islands to carry out road repair and construction, renovation of school buildings and other public facilities, medical work in outlying areas, and on-the-job training in construction skills for local trainees.

At the close of fiscal year 1970, active Army Special Forces consisted of six groups and one separate company located in Germany, Okinawa, Thailand, Vietnam, and the Canal Zone and in the continental United States at Fort Devens, Massachusetts, and Fort Bragg, North Carolina.

In the Republic of Vietnam the 5th Special Forces Group continued its mission of advising the Vietnamese Special Forces and managing the Civilian Irregular Defense Group program under which indigenous forces, commanded by Vietnamese Special Forces, conducted extensive operations against enemy infiltration routes in remote peripheral areas. Other activities, such as psychological operations, engineer construction for camp and community, and military civic actions, continued to contribute to the internal stability of areas where Civilian Irregular Defense Group camps are located.

In Thailand, the 46th Special Forces Company continued its successful work with the Thai Army and other government agencies to assist that country in its internal security operations against Communist-inspired insurgency.

In the Panama Canal Zone the 8th Special Forces Group continued regional training assistance to Central and South American countries. While the value of such assistance to friendly foreign governments is well established, reduction of units in the Canal Zone appears likely.

The 3d Special Forces Group was inactivated in December 1969 at Fort Bragg. Although Special Forces units may well be affected by Army reductions in the post-Vietnam period, they are capable of providing military advisory assistance with minimum forces, and would be used in connection with requests from friendly foreign countries on the basis of justification and availability.

Attention was centered during the year upon providing Special Forces units with a more viable organizational structure; new tables of organization and equipment approved in May 1970 were more closely geared to current missions and will be instituted in fiscal year 1971.

The Special Action Forces, originally formed in 1963 by the attachment of engineer, medical, intelligence, psychological operations, civil affairs, military police, and signal elements to a nucleus Special Forces Group, were reduced to four during the year. One was oriented toward Asia, one toward Europe, one toward Latin America, and the fourth toward Africa, the Middle East, and South Asia. Mobile training and technical advisory team activities formed the bulk of their operations during the year. In Latin America, thirteen countries received assistance ranging from radio maintenance work in Panama to water purification training in Venezuela.

Military Assistance

The Army's military assistance responsibility includes funding, training, logistic support, and production. In fiscal year 1970 the Military Assistance Program (MAP) continued the rapid decline that began in 1966. The Department of Defense requested $430 million in new funds, and Congress appropriated $350 million and imposed a similar limit on 1971 new obligational authority. The Army's portion of the appropriation was $208 million. The size of the appropriation reflects the competing demands between domestic programs and the war in Vietnam, along with increasing congressional opposition to military assistance and other oversea commitments. Along this line the Army has supported the national goal of replacing grant aid with military sales. Meanwhile, the 1970 Military Assistance Service Funded program remained at the $2.1 billion level of the previous year. It was anticipated that the Vietnamization program would increase this amount slightly in 1971.

An amendment to the Foreign Assistance Act of 1969 restricted the number of foreign students who may be trained in the United States in a year to a number no greater than the total of foreign civilians brought to the United States under the Mutual Educational and Cultural Exchange Act of 1961 in the preceding year. The restriction applies only to MAP grant aid, and required a 13 percent reduction in foreign military personnel who would have come to the United States under that program during fiscal year 1970.

The foreign military training program of about $20 million operated in more than seventy countries during the year. The U.S. government received about $2.5 million for foreign military sales training, and these funds supported approximately 10,650 training spaces in the United States and 7,320 overseas, along with orientation tours for 679 senior military personnel, 17 mobile training teams, and 65 field training service personnel.

Army-furnished training to support the Vietnamization program increased substantially in fiscal year 1970, with increases particularly noticeable in artillery, signal, and ordnance training spaces. Civilian university training spaces, both graduate and undergraduate, were increased from thirty-one to sixty-four. The major increase was for the Republic of Vietnam Air Force. About 1,100 pilots entered training in the United States, including English language courses and the special pilot courses at Fort Wolters, Texas, and Fort Stewart, Georgia. About 355 aviation mechanics were trained at Fort Eustis, Virginia. The Vietnamese pilot training program was expected to continue at a somewhat reduced rate in 1971.

Communications-Electronics

In a period of ever-increasing use of the world's airwaves by all nations, the operation of communications and electronic equipment of all kinds and under all conditions, including wartime, is a matter of general concern. During fiscal year 1970, the U.S. Army undertook for the first time to analyze the communications-electronic environment that would result from the deployment, by all participants including potential opposing forces, of an estimated 220,000 emitting components, which is considered to be the situation that will be faced in the 1975 period. The purpose of the analysis was to determine the extent to which U.S. Army communications, operating in a worldwide environment, might cause or be subjected to interference. The results of this investigation will be used on a long-range basis to guide the development of communications-electronics systems.

Because of the expanding use of the world's airwaves for both military and commercial purposes, communications discipline and economy have become increasingly important. Three general themes have been stressed in the U.S. Army's communications management program: efficient and effective use of existing facilities to preclude unnecessary expansion; proper and maximum utilization of government equipment to hold leasing of commercial facilities to a minimum; and provision to the commander of the equipment he needs to accomplish his mission. Among continuing economy and discipline measures, special emphasis was given during the past year to control of voice communications.

In a day of complex, technical, and far-flung communications-electronics systems and equipment, efficient and effective operation at all levels requires active and sustained management. There were a number of management activities during fiscal year 1970 that were more than routine. Communications-electronics management in Army installations in the United States, for example, was addressed in a major study, and one of the important recommendations, approved by the Chief of Staff, was that the installation's communications-electronics officer should be at the principal staff level. As a member of the installation's principal staff, the C-E officer will be in a position to evaluate communications-electronics requirements and provide support expeditiously. This management improvement will be reflected not only at installation level but in more responsive communications Army-wide.

The first communications systems program review was held at Fort Monmouth, New Jersey, on October 21–22, 1969. Limited in scope to tactical communications, it produced a concept of a master plan that would address all aspects of management of tactical communications systems on an integrated systems basis. This program includes all communications from the squad radio of the combat zones to complex multichannel tropospheric scatter and ground satellite communications assemblages, which constitute the nerve cells for the Army in the field. The initial master plan was developed as a low-cost, in-house effort. It includes an overview of Army goals, priorities for development and procurement, impact statements for determination of trade-offs required by budgetary and manpower constraints, data elements such as force planning guidance, and concepts and doctrine for employment.

The tactical multichannel communications system provides facilities to connect command and area signal centers. These centers have telephone, message, and data facilities which are tied together by multichannel radio and cable transmission facilities. The signal centers are located throughout theater Army and field Army down to and including brigade headquarters and firing batteries in the air defense artillery. The equipment used in this system provides voice, record, and data communications circuits required for command, control, and logistic purposes. Multichannel means of communications conserve manpower, equipment, and available radio frequency spectrums by combining several communications channels for transmission over one radio.

Multichannel equipment using a digital technique for transmission is now being introduced in the field. Approximately 25 percent of the active Army requirement for transmission equipment had been fielded through fiscal year 1970. For the most part, the equipment is solid state and represents the latest technological state of the art. It is smaller, lighter, easier to maintain, and more reliable than older equipment, provides greater channel capacity, and is more mobile and responsive than the equipment being replaced.

In other branches of the communications-electronics field, management review and improvement actions were stressed in an Army-wide audio-visual activities program and in an Army avionics master plan, the former embracing photographic and television mediums, the latter the application of electronics to aviation and astronautics. Because of the ever-widening military use of television for training, safety, security, morale, and briefing, new policy and standards in television utilization were issued during the year. Distribution control of motion pictures was also tightened.

The rapid expansion of U.S. forces in Vietnam beginning in 1966 required a comparable buildup of communications units. Between April 1966, when the 1st Signal Brigade was activated in Vietnam, and mid-1968 the brigade grew from an organization of three groups and eight battalions to five groups and twenty-two battalions. Numerous problems grew out of the expansion: skill authorizations and requirements were thrown out of balance; companies were cross-assigned among battalions; and operating units were performing housekeeping in fixed facilities. In general, unit authorization documents were out of line with the actual mission, organization, personnel, and equipment. To rectify the command, control, and organizational problems and provide the mixture of fixed communications facilities and mobile tactical elements required by the combat situation, the 1st Signal Brigade was reorganized effective March 1, 1970. A streamlined and efficient force compatible with the increased tempo of the war was structured at no increase in authorized strength or equipment.

In September 1968 the Department of the Army initiated a special study—Communications Evaluation in Southeast Asia—to analyze communications activities there during the period 1964–68. The final report was a comprehensive examination of important communications details in Southeast Asia, covering concepts and doctrine, force development, materiel requirements, communications standards, and management. The Army Staff evaluation of the study led to corrective actions, most of which were completed by the close of the fiscal year. Several matters bearing upon joint doctrine for communications in the communications zone and theater area remained to be resolved at year's end.

Project Mallard, the quadripartite research, development, and procurement program intended to provide a secure tactical communications system for American, British, Canadian, and Australian forces in the 1980's, entered the concept formulation phase in the first half of the fiscal year, until in December 1969 the U.S. Senate-House Conference Committee on Defense Appropriations recommended that discontinuation of the project be explored. A hold placed on U.S. contracts was still in effect at year's end, severely restricting U.S. participation in the project.

Civil Defense

The civil defense program is an essential and prudent component of U.S. strategic defensive forces. It is insurance in the event the U.S. deterrent fails or an attack is accidentally launched. Defense Department studies show that in large-scale nuclear attacks, a nationwide fallout shelter system has a greater lifesaving potential per dollar invested than any other single element of strategic defense. Therefore, primary focus in civil defense continued to be the development of a nationwide fallout shelter system for the entire population, whether at home, work, or school. Management of this and supporting emergency systems was accomplished through the dual use of existing capabilities of state and local governments.

Civil defense worked on a day-to-day basis with the governments of each of the states, the District of Columbia, Puerto Rico, American Samoa, Guam, the Virgin Islands, the Canal Zone, and thousands of local jurisdictions. Many organizations, community leaders, and individuals supported these efforts. There were about 4,500 local jurisdictions, representing more than 89 percent of the nation's population, involved directly with the OCD (Office of Civil Defense) in the nationwide civil defense program.

Fiscal year 1970 was the ninth year of continuous development of a nationwide fallout shelter system. Although fund restrictions have been increasingly severe since fiscal year 1966, the civil defense capability today would make a major contribution to the protection of the population in the event of a large-scale nuclear attack. Civil defense programs have also provided trained personnel and workable emergency plans which have been used in various peacetime disasters. By the end of the fiscal year, approximately 197.3 million fallout shelter spaces, with a protection factor (PF) of 40 or better, had been located through various surveys. PF expresses the relation between the amounts of radiation that would be received by an unprotected person and a person inside the shelter. Thus, an unprotected person would receive 40 times more radiation than the person inside a shelter with a PF of 40.

Survey and inventory of public shelter space are conducted by the U.S. Army Corps of Engineers and the U.S. Naval Facilities Engineering Command. The Defense Supply Agency provides logistic support to the OCD public fallout shelter stocking program. By year's end the fallout shelter inventory showed 202,298 facilities with public fallout protected space for 194.8 million people. About 128 million of these spaces were licensed, 108 million marked with shelter signs, and 63.8 million stocked with federal supplies sufficient to sustain occupants for fourteen days or, if shelter areas were filled to their rated capacities, over 103.4 million occupants for eight days. Warehouse stocks of shelter supplies were essentially exhausted during fiscal year 1970. Federally furnished standard survival supplies for additional shelters must await further appropriations.

The Office of Civil Defense, with the assistance of universities, institutes, and professional societies, has qualified 19,843 architects and engineers in the technology of fallout shelter design and analysis. These architects and engineers through the application of appropriate design techniques are able to incorporate additional fallout protection in new buildings at little or no additional cost. The Office of Civil Defense also offers professional advisory services to architects and their clients through the professional advisory service centers established at forty-four universities.

The Direct Mail Shelter Development System (DMSDS) that was functioning in forty-four states at the end of the fiscal year is essentially a systematic procedure for contacting and encouraging architects and owners of proposed buildings to use design techniques that provide fallout protection. By June 30, 1970, 304,550 construction reports had been reviewed; 19,409 of these had been processed and mailed covering projects located in the forty-four states. Responses indicating co-operative interest were received for 7,300 projects, about 38 percent of the project mailing. Approximately 40 percent of those responding requested technical assistance. Results by the end of the fiscal year indicated that approximately 1,700 building projects valued at a total of more than $4.2 billion would yield 690,000 additional shelter spaces with architect and owner acceptance of DMSDS advice. The cost to the building owner would be approximately $6.50 per shelter space, representing about 0.1 percent of the total valuation of the building projects.

The Home Fallout Protection Survey was not conducted in fiscal year 1970 because the Census Bureau was totally involved with the decennial census. The 1970 census was expected to provide information about homes with basements. It is estimated that twenty-two million homes with basements have not been surveyed, and that these could yield significant protection for seventy-seven million occupants.

Community Shelter Planning (CSP) is another important aspect of the shelter program. CSP is designed to develop procedures in local communities for making efficient use of the best available protection against radioactive fallout and to provide information to the public on where to go and what to do in the event of an attack. CSP also identifies in geographic detail the unfilled requirements for fallout shelter. At the end of the fiscal year, CSP projects completed or in process covered 1,767 counties or planning areas with a total population of more than 126.2 million people.

The development of the following civil defense emergency operations systems was continued to help assure the effective use of shelters and the conduct of recovery operations: a nationwide warning system to alert people to impending attack and to direct them to shelters; communications systems to keep people informed and to enable officials to direct emergency operations; nationwide monitoring and reporting systems to collect, evaluate, and disseminate information on radiological fallout resulting from attack; and a damage assessment system to provide guidance for preattack planning and postattack operations.

Emergency operating centers (EOC's) are needed at the seat of government at all levels for effective executive direction and control in any widespread emergency. These EOC's are fallout-protected centers, planned, staffed, and provided with communications and warning facilities for key officials to use in directing emergency operations. By the end of the fiscal year, 1,270 state and local government EOC's were operational. In addition, there were 628

EOC's in planning, 640 under construction, 481 with construction completed, and 591 in the process of being equipped.

To permit broadcasting of information to the public from these EOC's, radio connections were in the process of being installed to protect commercial broadcast stations in the Emergency Broadcast System (EBS). The EBS was established to provide official information to the public in an attack emergency and can be activated only by the President. As part of this system, OCD has a broadcast station protection program to provide selected stations with fallout shelter, emergency power, and the radio links to EOC's. This enables key broadcast stations to remain on the air in a fallout environment. At the end of the fiscal year, 610 broadcast stations were included in the program.

All states and 4,500 local governments participating in the civil defense program submitted annual program papers, one of the requirements for eligibility to receive federal civil defense assistance. Federal assistance includes technical guidance, training and education, and surplus property donations, as well as financial assistance. To provide maximum assistance to U.S. citizens and full participation by civil defense, all restrictions were removed on the use of civil defense personnel, supplies, and equipment in peacetime disasters. The Civil Defense Education Program was modified to put new emphasis on incorporating civil defense into the secondary school curriculum, on developing school self-protection civil defense plans and programs, and on supplying shelter space in school facilities where needed.

Awareness and interest are essential to public support of civil defense emergency preparedness. To this end an information services office was established to provide information to all media concerning the day-to-day activities of the agency. A new liaison services office also serves this end by maintaining contact with business, industry, and organizations of various types.

Other civil defense supporting activities included research to develop an improved technical basis for program direction and guidance; warehousing and distribution of emergency supplies; prepositioning of emergency information to tell the public of actions to take in an emergency; activities and information to gain the participation of industry, national organizations, professional associations, institutions, and agencies; and liaison with other elements of the federal government and with civil defense authorities of friendly countries.

The Army has primary service responsibility for military support of civil defense functions within the continental United States.

All services recognize the need for and support a strong civil defense program and develop survival and recovery programs for the armed forces. The services represent a major source of assistance to civil authorities in civil defense activities because of their organization, specialized equipment, disciplined manpower, and long experience in dealing with emergencies.

The Commanding General, U.S. Continental Army Command, and continental U.S. (CONUS) Army commanders provide planning guidance to the CONUS state adjutants general who, while in preattack state status, prepare military support of civil defense plans for each state. The adjutants general, when called to federal service as state area commanders, exercise operational control over military units made available for transattack and postattack military support of civil defense missions. In Alaska, Hawaii, and Puerto Rico, similar military support of civil defense planning and operations arrangements are the responsibility of the appropriate unified command commander and the adjutant general.

The Army, with Department of Defense approval, is authorized to establish civil defense reinforcement training units (RTU's) with members drawn from the Individual Ready Reserve. RTU's are authorized to perform preattack planning and training in either civil defense or military support of civil defense. Members earn retirement point credit for such participation.

III. The War in Vietnam

Operations

U.S. Army forces in South Vietnam were substantially reduced as the result of presidential decisions announced on June 8, September 16, and December 15, 1969. Almost 59,000 Army troops and 4 major units were redeployed, reducing Army strength there to less than 310,000. As noted above, 2 brigades of the 9th Infantry Division, a brigade of the 82d Airborne Division, the entire 1st Infantry Division, and a brigade of the 4th Infantry Division were withdrawn, the equivalent of 2⅓ divisions, leaving 6 division force equivalents in Vietnam at year's end.

On April 20, 1970, the President announced that within a year 150,000 more troops would be withdrawn. Subsequently, it was announced that an increment of 50,000 would be removed by October 15, and as the year ended, steps were in progress to carry out this decision.

The organization and disposition of the U.S. Army in Vietnam was progressively modified to meet the changing force levels and the gradual assumption of battlefield responsibility by the South Vietnamese. In some of the first adjustments, redeployment of the 1st and 2d Brigades of the 9th Infantry Division from the IV Corps Tactical Zone gave the Republic of Vietnam primary control of military operations in the Mekong Delta.

Redeployment of the 3d Marine Division with a proportionate share of logistical support from I Corps changed the balance between Army and Marine Corps forces in that area. The combat capability of the Marines was reduced from a level of more than twenty maneuver battalions to less than ten. On March 9, 1970, Headquarters, XXIV U.S. Army Corps, assumed responsibility for all U.S. forces in the I Corps Tactical Zone, including the III Marine Amphibious Force headquarters.

An important change in the Army's logistical structure took place in the consolidation of Headquarters, 1st Logistical Command, with Headquarters, U.S. Army, Vietnam, a move prompted by the decreasing presence of American forces in Vietnam, and one that contributed to the over-all strength reduction.

On the battlefield, Army forces operated in the I, II, and III Corps Tactical Zones, with IV Corps area operations passing to the

Vietnamese forces upon the departure of the 9th Division. U.S. units maintained pressure on the North Vietnamese and Viet Cong main force units, accelerated the pacification program, and concentrated upon the Vietnamization program.

Friendly forces maintained the initiative over the enemy main forces, capitalizing on superior firepower and mobility. Wide-ranging spoiling attacks, penetration of enemy base areas, and the capture of supply caches kept the enemy off balance, although he continued to demonstrate the ability to mount co-ordinated actions throughout South Vietnam. His casualties continued to run well above those of the allies.

The effect of tactical operations dating from 1965 was to force the enemy to seek sanctuary behind neutral borders in Cambodia and Laos. He continued to mount operations from these secure areas into South Vietnam at a time and place of his own choosing. In May and June 1970, combined U.S. and Republic of Vietnam forces moved against these enemy sanctuary areas in Cambodia. Huge stocks of supplies were captured and numerous bases and positions destroyed, seriously compromising the enemy's capability to launch operations into South Vietnam.

Several instances involving allegations of serious battlefield misconduct came to light during the year. One incident, involving operations around Son My (My Lai) in March 1968 in which noncombatants were alleged to have been killed, came to departmental attention in April 1969, at which time the Army opened an extensive investigation of the charges. In addition to investigations by the Inspector General and by military police criminal investigators, the Secretary of the Army and the Chief of Staff designated Lieutenant General William R. Peers to conduct an inquiry to determine why the matter was not disclosed at the time it was alleged to have occurred.

As the year closed, thirteen individuals still on active duty had been charged with committing crimes against persons or property in Son My on March 16, 1968. Charges against one of these were dismissed for insufficient evidence, and except for one case at Fort Hood, Texas, and one at Fort Benning, Georgia, the remaining cases were in various stages of judicial proceedings at Third Army headquarters, Fort McPherson, Georgia.

In addition to these cases, twelve officers were charged with failing to report or attempting to conceal the alleged incident. Disposition of these cases was consolidated at First Army headquarters, Fort Meade, Maryland. Charges against three of the officers were dismissed, and a decision was pending as the year closed concerning whether to order formal preliminary investigations in the remaining cases, as required under Article 32 of the Uniform Code of Military Justice.

The investigations also indicated that a number of former soldiers, now civilians, might be implicated in the case. A legal study was under way to determine whether criminal action might be taken against these former soldiers.

In another instance, the so-called Green Beret case, an Army investigation was conducted in July 1969 concerning the alleged death of a Vietnamese male near Nha Trang, Vietnam, on June 20, 1969. As a result of this investigation, charges of murdering and conspiring to murder a suspected agent were preferred against the commanding officer of the 5th Special Forces Group, six of his officers, and one of his noncommissioned officers. In August 1969 a formal pretrial investigation of the charges was conducted pursuant to Article 32 of the Uniform Code of Military Justice, and on September 22 the Commanding General of Support Troops, U.S. Army, Vietnam, referred the charges against six of the officers to trial by general court-martial, in which the maximum possible sentence was dismissal from the service, forfeiture of all pay and allowance, and life imprisonment. Charges against the remaining two were held in abeyance. On September 29, 1969, the Secretary of the Army assumed jurisdiction and ordered the charges against all accused dismissed. This action was taken because the Central Intelligence Agency, although not directly involved in the alleged incident, determined in the interest of national security that it would make none of its personnel available as witnesses in the trials. Since the accused would require the appearance of some of these witnesses, the Secretary of the Army concluded that a fair trial would not be possible.

Against the background of these cases, the Army reviewed its prisoner of war policies. The regulation providing for annual mandatory training for all Army personnel in the Geneva and Hague conventions relating to prisoner of war treatment was revised and expanded. Stress was placed upon the legal and tactical requirements for humane treatment of enemy military and civilian personnel, including the protection of their property; upon the distinction between legal and illegal orders; upon rules of engagement; and upon war crime reporting procedures. Instruction was to be presented by legally qualified personnel together with combat-experienced commanders. Practical training was to be integrated in tactical training exercises.

During the period covered by this report the U.S. Army continued to provide the bulk of the equipment to support Republic of Vietnam forces numbering over a million men. The flow was regulated by Vietnam's ability to receive, operate, maintain, and store materiel. Instruction in operation, administration, logistics, and training methods was productive, as was on-the-job training with experienced advisory and operating unit personnel in the field.

Progress in the Vietnamization program became more and more apparent. Vietnamese forces carried out an increasing number of operations, both day and night, some in areas beyond their previous zones of operation. Their dependence on U.S. support was considerably lessened. The operations in Cambodia provided valuable training as well as combat experience and enhanced the combat effectiveness of the Republic of Vietnam forces while paving the way for further U.S. redeployments. As the year closed, Republic of Vietnam forces held operational responsibility for the demilitarized zone separating the two Vietnams, for much of the inland provinces of the II Corps area, for Saigon, and for all of the IV Corps region. This shift in responsibility and the speed and size of U.S. troop withdrawals testified to the success and promise of the Vietnamization program.

Under the pacification program, the United States continued to advise and support Vietnamese efforts to establish security, stabilize and restore local government, and foster social and economic action to unify public support of the national government. The year's goals were to improve territorial security, protect against terrorism, expand the self-defense capability of the people, improve local administration, ameliorate the effects of the war on the individual citizen, inform the people, and in general raise the standard of living for all. Some of these aims were difficult to achieve. Good progress was made in local self-defense and administration and basic social reform. Overoptimism rather than lack of concern explained some of the shortcomings in the program.

Two U.S. Army civil affairs companies and four platoons operated in Vietnam during the 1970 fiscal year period, chiefly at province and district levels, contributing to the over-all pacification effort by conducting water surveys, providing medical and dental care, assisting refugees, constructing schools and sanitary facilities, providing agricultural advice, and handling foreign claims. Two Army engineer construction advisory detachments continued to support the Republic of Vietnam government's rural development program by providing assistance in numerous projects such as repairing dwellings, building roads, schools, dispensaries, and water systems, and in various other construction and self-help projects. And Army surgical teams continued to work in provincial hospitals, supporting the Republic of Vietnam Ministry of Public Health by providing medical care for civilians, furnishing advice and assistance in public health and sanitation, and training Vietnamese personnel in these areas.

Logistics

Over the past several years the United States and other Free World forces in Vietnam have had an overwhelming superiority in firepower, mobility, and communications. A high rate of operational readiness for nearly all types of equipment, and an equally high rate of availability of supplies attest to the effectiveness of the logistic support system. This is true despite the fact that these forces had large quantities of sophisticated and complex equipment and were operating in a remote and relatively primitive environment at the end of an attenuated line of communication. There were no embarrassing shortages of ammunition, fuel, or weapons. Ground and air assaults mounted from base camps dotting the countryside were supported by logistic complexes at Long Binh, Cam Ranh Bay, Qui Nhon, and Da Nang, with their computerized depots and deep draft ports.

In 1967, as logistic support operations improved, emphasis was placed increasingly on improving management practices and standards. Substantial progress was made in reducing field stock levels by relying on efficient transportation systems to meet urgent needs and by achieving greater accuracy in stock accounting and inventory. The Joint Logistics Review Board, established in Washington in March 1969, reviewed logistic operations through succeeding months to identify important lessons for the future.

In the field of transportation, the transition from expansion to retrenchment, reduction, and relocation of military operations raised a need for new management ideas and techniques rather than new hardware. The more noteworthy concepts in being or in prospect were the so-called "inventory in motion" control over shipments, closed loop and direct delivery techniques, the use of economical or routine airlift for selected items, and expanded use of containerization.

About 48 percent of all Army-sponsored cargo and 23 percent of the passengers moved during the year were transported to and from Southeast Asia. The Military Sea Transportation Service moved 7,594,200 measurement tons into the area, down by about 1,528,000 from the previous fiscal year. Cargo shipped by air totaled 141,600 short tons, down by about 79,900 from the previous year. Of the totals, 5,113,300 measurement tons were shipped by surface and 91,600 short tons by air from the continental United States.

During the fiscal year 387,692 passengers were moved from the continental United States to support operations in Southeast Asia, 387,600 by air and 92 by surface. Over 91,700 were moved within the theater.

Various expediting procedures were used to move essential equipment by airlift, perhaps the best known being the Red Ball express, established in 1965 to move critical spare parts and other essential items to repair deadlined equipment. Over 56,000 short tons of cargo were airlifted by this means between December 8, 1965, and June 30, 1969. About 10,000 short tons were delivered in fiscal year 1970.

As the year closed the Army was using nine ports in South Vietnam: Newport, Qui Non, Cam Ranh Bay, Vung Tau, Vung Ro, Cat Lai, Nha Be, and Nha Trang, all deep draft ports, and Phan Rang, a shallow draft port. Dong Tam, a shallow draft port in the Mekong Delta, which had supported the 9th Division, was closed in October 1969 as the division departed. Port congestion was no longer a problem. The average time a ship waited for a berth in Vietnam ports declined from 20.4 days in the critical 1965 period to an average of 1.5 days in 1970. The deep draft ports attained a daily throughput capacity of 25,000 short tons. Quarterly throughput—discharge and outload combined—in Army-operated ports in South Vietnam decreased by about 185,000 short tons compared to fiscal year 1969. During fiscal year 1970 the average ranged from 565,000 short tons in the opening quarter to 601,000 in the closing quarter, as opposed to 807,000 and 728,000 for the corresponding quarters in fiscal year 1969. The decrease was the result of reduced tonnages rather than handling capacity, another reflection of the leveling off in the theater.

Operation of the Saigon commercial port was turned over to the Republic of Vietnam Army during the year. Military cargo destined for U.S. forces in the Saigon area was consigned to Newport for discharge, and military assistance cargo was discharged exclusively at Saigon. To accomplish these arrangements, port designator codes were developed to control shipping and cargo storage, schedules were adjusted to permit fewer ships with larger loads, and Agency for International Development cargo was removed from the Department of Defense transportation system.

Vietnamization of the Saigon port began with on-the-job training of Republic of Vietnam Army personnel in the 65-foot tugs of the U.S. Harbor Craft Company, the tugs that move barges and berth oceangoing vessels. Personnel were trained in harbor towing, docking and undocking, rigging and inspecting tows, firefighting, diesel engine operation and maintenance, use of drill presses and other power tools, welding, and care and safety practices. There was training in crane operation and in port and terminal maintenance and salvage work, and some trainees were integrated into pier operation and cargo disposition, clearance, and planning. Thus by January 1970, the Republic of Vietnam Army assumed responsibility for discharge and backloading of all cargo arriving at the port of Saigon. Training in landing craft operation was conducted at Vung Tau, covering all echelons of maintenance connected with these craft.

To reduce average port hold times and increase handling efficiency, procedures for handling high priority cargo at aerial ports were revised so that super-priority cargo would not be delayed more than forty-eight hours. The concept was introduced at all continental U.S. aerial ports of embarkation and at twenty-one Air Force offshore stations in January 1970. Port times were considerably reduced at all reporting stations.

Ammunition procurement in fiscal year 1970 was designed to meet Southeast Asia and training requirements and leave sufficient stocks at the end of the funded delivery period to meet minimum needs. The ability of the ammunition production base to accelerate would protect against shortfall. The projected availability of ammunition was based on the assumption that consumption in Southeast Asia would be gradually reduced. Despite the fact that consumption rates varied during the year, no critical shortages were experienced. Where stocks were not adequate enough to meet competing demands, the Department of the Army Allocation Committee, Ammunition, controlled the distribution to U.S. Army and Free World forces, based upon consumption rates and stockage objectives within priorities established by the Army Chief of Staff. Ammunition for Republic of Vietnam Army forces was allocated and distributed in accordance with rates and stockage objectives approved by the Joint Chiefs of Staff.

As U.S. troop withdrawals from Vietnam began in the first quarter of the fiscal year, and with continuing redeployments in prospect, control over the redistribution of equipment became increasingly important. Department of the Army policy guidance stressed that scarce items should be kept under centralized control, while control over other supplies and materiel should be decentralized It was desirable to minimize redistribution costs by making full use of requirements in Vietnam and the Pacific region. Thus the majority of items were retained in Vietnam, although some shipments were made to U.S. forces in Europe.

The depot maintenance program for U.S. Army, Pacific, in fiscal years 1969 and 1970 was funded at $36 and $46 million respectively, more than double that of 1968. By performing depot maintenance within the command area, the maintenance cycle is shortened, transportation costs and pipeline requirements are reduced, and labor costs are substantially lower. It was possible to repair unserviceable equipment in the Far East that would have been washed out of the system through excessive cost had it been returned to the United States. The work has been done in Japan, Korea, Okinawa, and Taiwan.

In December 1969 a Vietnam asset reconciliation procedure was developed to cope with the problem of reconciling major item requirements and assets in U.S. Army, Vietnam. The concept recognized that units in Vietnam had equipment requirements that had never been formally documented in the authorization system, and that in many instances excess equipment was being used to satisfy real but undocumented requirements. Unit commanders were encouraged to report their actual assets. Those which can be applied against formal authorizations are reported through the regular unit reporting system. Assets on hand in excess of formal authorizations are reported to U.S. Army, Vietnam, where they are recorded in a special account and placed back on loan to the reporting unit. As of June 30, 1970, about $70 million in unreported assets had been accounted for under the new procedure.

Current and projected budget restrictions and force reductions in the Pacific, with attendant reductions in equipment densities, clearly indicated early in fiscal year 1970 that logistical operations should be reorganized and realigned. Thus in August 1969 the first phase of the Master Logistic Plan covering the decade 1970–80 was launched. Initial features included a single requisition pipeline for U.S., Vietnamese, and Free World Military Assistance Forces and a central control facility to integrate fiscal and supply management. A central control facility will be established on Okinawa to perform supply management, programing, and budgeting for all Army elements in northeast and southeast Asia. The inventory control centers in Thailand, Vietnam, and Korea were to be eliminated and their supply management functions assumed by the central control facility. Existing U.S. Army depots in Vietnam and Korea were to be phased down to field depot level and stock only those fast-moving items justified by demand. Depots in Japan and Thailand were to be reduced to installation supply activity level. The 2d Logistical Command on Okinawa was to become an advance depot.

Ultimately, all requisitions for U.S., Vietnamese, and Free World Military Assistance forces were to be processed through the central control facility, which will maintain logistic and financial management data, develop reports and budgets, and maintain consumption factors by types of forces. Among the anticipated net improvements from the near term portion of the Master Logistics Plan were reductions of inventories, of supplies in the pipeline, and of logistic support forces, as well as improved logistic support organization and financial control.

Under the Vietnamization program, the equipment status was favorable throughout the year, with the supply of essential items in phase with Republic of Vietnam Army unit activation schedules. Vietnamese logistic management and technical service schools trained increasing numbers of students, and, to keep up with the expanding requirement for trained personnel, an on-the-job training program was begun. This program was enlarged from 37 students in 3 courses in April 1969 to 1,500 students in 226 courses as the year closed, and such training was employed in all indigenous logistic commands.

In another move to further Vietnamese logistic self-sufficiency, the U.S. Military Assistance Command and Vietnamese armed forces representatives developed a program to improve Republic of Vietnam Army rebuild depots. By perfecting depot facilities, equipment status, and technical capability, indigenous agencies would be able to carry out efficient repair operations and reduce the amount of materiel shipped out of Vietnam for repair.

Materiel management efforts focused on effective utilization of equipment and supplies in Southeast Asia. As U.S. forces withdraw, their resources are made available to satisfy Republic of Vietnam Army requirements. Shipments from the United States were limited to certain critical items, and U.S. and Republic of Vietnam Army needs were met to a large extent from supplies already on hand in Southeast Asia.

Facilities as well as supplies have been or are to be transferred to Vietnamese control. In the fall of 1969, the Army began developing plans and procedures for the transfer of real and related property. During the fiscal year, as U.S. forces began evacuating certain areas, transfers took place, the Dong Tam base camp heading the list.

The size of the U.S. Army force in Vietnam suggests the magnitude of the task of redistributing equipment that attends with-drawal of Army elements. The prospect of massive turn-ins of materiel by redeploying units, some being inactivated and thus not needing to retain equipment, raised the problem of how to inspect, segregate, reallocate, and move the large quantities involved.

Normally a complete and time-consuming technical inspection by qualified mechanics would be performed on each item of equip-ment to determine its condition and earmark it for a specific level of maintenance. Because of the magnitude of the task in Vietnam, such procedures would retard progress. Consequently, in Septem-ber 1969 a procedure labeled Special Criteria for Retrograde of Army Materiel (SCRAM) was developed—a simplified inspection-classification system that involves a visual check of an item for missing or damaged parts and for over-all condition. Instituted in October 1969, this procedure was used to classify materiel becom-ing available as a result of troop redeployment.

Engineer Operations

The engineer force in Vietnam was reduced in fiscal year 1970 from 36,000 to about 30,000 personnel. Most engineer troop activ-ity was devoted to operational and combat support. The troop effort comprised 14 percent in military construction, 47 percent in airfield and road construction, and 39 percent in operational and combat support.

Engineer units in Vietnam were heavily engaged in Vietnami-zation activities. Engineer equipment with an aggregate value of over $7.5 million was transferred to Vietnamese engineer units. An active affiliation between Vietnamese and U.S. engineer units produced marked improvement in indigenous organization during the year.

Engineer troop activity continued in Thailand. Work progressed on eighty-seven kilometers of highway in northeast Thailand to pro-vide a supply route to the air base at Nakhon Phonom, and a 2,000-man cantonment area was completed on the Gulf of Thailand midway between the Sattahip port complex and the Utapao air base.

Perhaps the most significant engineer construction activity in Vietnam was the lines of communication program. Initiated in 1966, it provides for a network of modern high-speed highways connecting population centers and strategic areas in South Vietnam. The over-all objectives of the LOC program are to support tactical operations by providing routes for the safe movement of materiel and fire support; accelerate the pacification program by opening up previously inaccessible areas to military forces; and stimulate the economic development of the country by promoting the free movement of foods and goods from farm and factory to market.

The LOC program calls for improving national and interprovincial highways to provide an all-weather, two-lane, class-50 road network extending from the demilitarized zone to the Mekong Delta. The total length of the system is about 4,100 kilometers. The Army's portion of the program (the U.S. Navy is responsible for 425 kilometers) is being carried out by a combination of troop and contractor effort, and during the 1971 fiscal year Republic of Vietnam Army construction units will assume responsibility for 165 kilometers. U.S. Army engineer troops will thus construct something over 2,400 kilometers of roads, and contractor crews will complete the remaining 1,100 kilometers.

This LOC program utilizes somewhere between 40 and 50 percent of the U.S. Army engineer capacity in Vietnam. Its magnitude is demonstrated by the fact that the road-building job is the equivalent of constructing a two-lane highway from Washington, D.C., to Las Vegas, Nevada. By June 30, 1970, about 1,700 kilometers of highway had been completed by troop and contractor effort. To expedite the program, the Army purchased and sent to Vietnam commercial construction equipment worth about $20 million. This shipment marked the first time that off-the-shelf commercial equipment was used without modification or military standardization.

In this connection, a departmental policy letter on providing construction units with commercial equipment was published. The objectives of the policy are to meet Army requirements for construction equipment more promptly; insure that the equipment is of the latest design; reduce the variety of end items and repair parts; procure and support commercial equipment and systems at the lowest life-cycle cost; insure that it meets performance, maintenance, and support requirements before being issued to troops; provide for disposal of materiel; and in general insure that construction equipment is available, reliable, maintainable, adaptable, and versatile. It is anticipated that present plans will be approved and the first commercial equipment fielded during 1971.

The Viet Cong and North Vietnamese continued to employ widespread nuisance mining in South Vietnam during the year. As a result, Army engineers devoted a lot of time and effort to clearing miles of communications routes used by friendly forces. In mine warfare the advantage tends to rest with the party doing the mining, because of options of time, place, and method. In the past year, a lot of attention was centered on countering this threat.

The more effective solution is one that integrates individual and unit training, denial and surveillance measures, and detection and neutralization hardware and techniques. In the individual training area, basic combat trainees at the Army Training Center, Fort Lewis, Washington, were given countermine warfare instruction concurrently with the basic courses. In South Vietnam, units developed integrated programs geared to the specific threats they were encountering; tank-mounted mine-clearing rollers and tunnel and mine detection dogs were both used successfully. The mine problem was also recognized in budget actions at the departmental level.

The Army's engineer laboratories also developed shelters for parked aircraft. New designs for protective revetment to counter blast and fragmentation damage to aircraft on Southeast Asia airfields consist of a thin-walled soil bin about a foot thick with a wall structure using several optional revetting materials including used landing mat. These designs are economical in construction time and effort and practical in terms of the level of protection required.

From the foregoing it will be seen that numerous actions were in progress during the year to reduce U.S. participation in the Vietnam War. Troop levels were substantially reduced. Combat responsibilities were being gradually transferred to the Republic of Vietnam. Indigenous forces were supplied with increasing quantities of equipment and trained in its use, and logistic adjustments between U.S. and Republic of Vietnam forces, involving supplies, equipment, transportation, maintenance and repair, port and base operation, and property, were in progress as the year closed.

IV. Force Development

Fiscal year 1970 was a period of appreciable adjustment in Army force posture. Most of the elements withdrawn from Vietnam were inactivated, as were other supporting units of various types in the United States. Strength in terms of active Army division forces worldwide fell from 19⅔ to 17⅓. There were corresponding reductions in military and civilian strengths as the Army sought to cut expenditures by $1 billion as part of a $3 billion reduction imposed upon the Department of Defense in October 1969.

Priorities were assessed worldwide and personnel reductions were keyed to base closures, adjustments in force levels, and modifications in priorities. A total of 17,441 direct hire civilian employees, both U.S. and foreign nationals, supporting military functions were released.

In December 1969 the President directed that the number of U.S. personnel in certain foreign countries be reduced by 10 percent from the level of June 30, 1969. The Army's target was established at 3,093 military personnel (excluding Vietnam) and 2,321 U.S. civilian employees, to be completed by June 1970. Some of the personnel released as a result of the October 1969 action were credited to this reduction.

In March 1970 the Secretary of Defense announced military and civilian manpower reductions within the United States. These reductions were geared to base closures, mission changes, lower training loads, and other actions that would make it possible for the Army to achieve its programed fiscal year 1970 end strength. This step involved reductions of 9,055 military and 6,414 civilian personnel. Headquarters activities shared in the personnel cuts. The departmental headquarters and certain class II field activities were assessed a 15 percent reduction, although in many instances the mission and work load remained unchanged despite the reduced staffing.

At the same time that mission and support activity resources were decreasing, there was an increase in the Army's contribution to federal programs to alleviate domestic problems and provide opportunities to the disadvantaged. Among these were the President's Stay-in-School Campaign and the program for summer employment of youth. The manpower and funds required to support these and other important programs had to be absorbed within the diminishing resource levels authorized to the Department of the Army.

The downward personnel trends emphasized the importance of manpower management. Priorities and allocations were under close review to insure that only essential functions and activities were continued.

Plans

Changes in personnel and fund authorizations, as well as in oversea commitments and the nature of external threats, give mobilization and contingency planning their evolutionary character. Various mixtures and sizes of military forces must be applied against existing or potential menaces and related to various locations around the world today and in the future.

In October 1969, new instructions were issued on the planning, programing, and budgeting system for the military services which introduced new procedures for developing the Five Year Defense Program. The projected availability of funds is used as the starting point in developing future programs, and the services, the Joint Chiefs of Staff, and separate agencies are given greater latitude in developing forces and materiel and supporting programs within the fiscal guidance. As the fiscal year closed, the Army was operating in the first annual cycle of the new system and there were indications that the development schedules of several Army plans would have to be changed.

The contingency planning process starts in the Joint Strategic Capabilities Plan, with the Joint Chiefs of Staff assigning major commanders to plan for certain contingencies. The major forces available for planning are listed in this document and in the Army Strategic Capabilities Plan, and include only existing forces. Both plans specify the contingencies for which either partial or full mobilization may be required. Commanders in turn list force requirements which may become the basis for mobilization planning.

The heart of contingency planning is the Joint Chiefs of Staff deployment reporting system, an automatic data processing system that facilitates emergency deployment or redeployment actions, one that is integrated into the worldwide military command and control system, in which the Army station is the Army Operations Center System. The deployment reporting system displays data for each type force required by a commander in a time-phased force deployment listing; provides the Army capability by unit to support the requirement; determines transportation requirements;

computes resupply requirements; and determines force routing of the unit.

The mobilization planning concept was recently redefined. A new annex, Force Mobilization Planning Guidance, was being added to the Army Strategic Capabilities Plan, incorporating guidance and direction needed by major commands to prepare their force mobilization plans to support contingency plans. Two major appendixes list mobilization, deployment, or redeployment data for units of all components, and U.S. Army, Europe, requirements and capabilities.

Organization

The methods and techniques of managing Army installations were advanced significantly during the year as a result of the findings and recommendations of an Army team that studied the operation of continental U.S. installations in the light of their support missions and investigated ways of improving them. The study disclosed that extensive differences had developed in installation staff organization—differences that were wide enough to invalidate comparisons of management techniques and program effectiveness. It was apparent that a standard organization with uniform titles and duties for principal managers was required if installation management was to be improved. The Army Staff developed and put into effect a standard organizational structure for industrial and community activities common to Army installations. Modifications were included to permit adaptations to combat units, schools, training centers, and other activities located on an installation. These modifications defer to considerations of economy by requiring Army tenant units to perform self support to the degree that is possible without inhibiting their primary functions and missions. By the year's close, thirty-eight installations were prepared to open the new fiscal year under the new standard structure, and other commands would be added as modifications were developed suitable to their individual situations.

An equipment survey program was established during the year under which equipment authorization and use in table of distribution and allowance units would be analyzed on-site at Army installations. A Defense Department requirement that major equipment authorizations be reviewed periodically was incorporated in the new survey program.

Training and Schooling

As a result of withdrawals from Vietnam and changes in fiscal year 1970 manpower programs, the Army's need for new soldiers diminished. The lower training requirement, coupled with fiscal constraints, dictated a corresponding reduction in the training base structure. Beginning in December 1969, the number of basic combat training companies was reduced from 560 to 460; infantry advanced individual training companies were reduced from 110 to 80 in January 1970. As a result of these and related reductions, training centers at Fort Benning, Georgia, and Fort Huachuca, Arizona, were closed while operations at Fort Gordon, Georgia, Fort McClellan, Alabama, Fort Bliss, Texas, and Fort Lewis, Washington, were curtailed. Further training base adjustments were in prospect for fiscal year 1971.

For those who enter military service with less than a fifth grade reading ability, a six-week Army preparatory training program is conducted at all basic combat training centers. Classes are conducted for 6 hours daily, with 120 hours devoted to reading, writing, and English, and 60 hours to social studies, citizenship, and arithmetic. Trainees achieving fifth grade equivalency by the third week move out of the program into regular basic combat training; others remain for the full six weeks. Over 23,000 trainees have entered the program since it began in April 1968. Of this number, over 15,000 were reading at the fifth grade level by the end of three weeks. Another 3,400 achieved the goal in six weeks, while the same number failed to reach the desired goal in the allotted period.

Based on field commanders' comments and a personal visit to Vietnam, the commanding general of the Continental Army Command found that there were certain areas in combat arms advanced individual training that required emphasis. Initial consideration of extending this training to ten weeks (from the existing nine weeks for infantry and eight for other combat arms trainees) was dropped because of budgetary and manpower constraints, and it was implemented on a pilot basis for infantry trainees only. The test was conducted at Fort McClellan from May to December 1969. In the initial course a twelve-day field training exercise was substituted for the standard ninety-hour exercise of the nine-week program. The purpose was to apply all training given in the early stages and prepare the participants for the continuous field duty that they would experience in Vietnam. Since training motivation was difficult to maintain over the extended period, and because of budget and manpower constraints, the program was cut back to nine weeks with a seven-day field exercise. The new program was instituted with the training cycle that began on February 24, 1970.

Training with the M16 rifle was introduced in March 1965 in

infantry advanced individual training at Fort Gordon. By April 1967 all live firing in Vietnam-oriented infantry training had been converted from the M14 to the M16 rifle, and in February 1968 full conversion was approved subject to the gradual availability of weapons following priority shipment to Vietnam. By March 1970 the last M14's were phased out and the M16's were in general use.

In September 1968 the Army Chief of Staff directed that foreign weapons training be integrated into Army programs, and by August 1969 this order had been carried out. In basic combat training the program consists of an orientation, a static display of the Russian AK47 and six other principal small arms used by the Viet Cong and North Vietnamese, and a training film covering the nomenclature, functioning, and tactical employment of these weapons. In advanced individual training the program varies, from familiarization instruction on loading and unloading procedures and live firing demonstrations of the AK47 to illustrate its selective firing capability and cyclic rate, to "crack and thump" training using the AK47 intermixed with U.S. weapons.

One technique that has had considerable impact on Army training concepts, manpower management, and the Army's ability to meet its important requirements in the E–5 and E–6 grades is the skill development base program. The purpose is to train individuals so that they will perform satisfactorily in their initial duty assignment; this instruction comes right after basic combat and advanced individual training and normally lasts twenty-one to twenty-four weeks. During fiscal year 1970 about 16,000 enlisted men were graduated from forty-five courses and promoted to either E–5 or E–6 under the program. Reports from commanders in Vietnam indicated that these men were doing well in combat.

In the field of military logistics, attention was centered on increasing the number of trained logistic personnel in the Army and insuring that skills were properly utilized with regard to Vietnam. Officer and enlisted courses were structured to meet a continuing need throughout the Pacific region for personnel trained in inventory control and depot operations. On a longer range basis, steps were being taken to develop a rotation and training base for the more critical logistic skills.

There was an increase in adviser training in the year. The Vietnam Training Center of the Foreign Service Institute trained selected majors to be district senior advisers in a tailored 18-week course, a companion to the 33-week province senior adviser course.

Aviation training output continued at a high level during the year. Almost 7,000 active Army pilots were trained, as were 207

U.S. Marine Corps and 163 foreign military students. And in October 1969 the Army also began to give helicopter pilot training at continental U.S. bases to Republic of Vietnam Air Force personnel, in a program designed to produce over 1,000 qualified pilots by June 1971.

In the field of schooling, the Continental Army Command began system engineering all officer candidate school (OCS) courses to eliminate repetition of subjects given during pre-OCS training or officer basic courses. Studies were in progress to determine whether advanced individual training was necessary prior to OCS, and whether OCS could be cut from twenty-three to eighteen weeks and all graduates sent to a basic officer course. Manpower cuts in the coming two fiscal years will require that one of the OCS schools be closed.

The Reserve Officers' Training Corps continued to be the largest and most economical source of new officers for both the regular Army and the Army Reserve. During fiscal year 1970, fifteen new host institutions began enrolling students in the ROTC program. Three institutions—Harvard and Boston Universities and Dartmouth College—elected to discontinue the program during the same period. In addition, the senior ROTC program at Allen Military Academy was terminated because the institution will no longer conduct instruction at the college level. Opening enrollments were down 41,000 over the previous year; over half of the decline was attributable to the conversion of the ROTC basic course from required to elective status at thirty-nine host institutions. The remainder of the decrease could probably be attributed to reduced draft pressure, talk of an all-volunteer Army, and antiwar, antimilitary activity. Dissident activity directed against ROTC increased considerably over the previous year; there were 346 incidents as compared with 85 in 1969. About half of 166 incidents that occurred in the period May 1–23, for example, involved acts of violence such as riot, arson, bombing, and assault.

The Army announced the award of 1,242 four-year scholarships to selected high school graduates in April 1970. These along with two- and three-year scholarships that were to be allocated in the summer of 1970 would bring the Army scholarship ceiling up to its authorized 5,500 level. The ROTC program produced 16,581 officers in fiscal year 1970.

During the year the Army Command and General Staff College established co-operative advanced degree programs with the University of Kansas, Kansas State University, and the University of Missouri (Kansas City). The Army War College established pilot advanced degree programs with Georgetown University and with Shippensburg State College of Pennsylvania.

Weapons Systems

When the President announced his decision on March 14, 1969, to proceed with the deployment of a limited ballistic missile defense system, designated as Safeguard, he conceived it to fulfill three basic objectives: protection of U.S. land-based retaliatory forces against a direct attack by the Soviet Union; defense of the American people against the kind of nuclear attack which Communist China is likely to be able to mount within the decade; and protection against the possibility of accidental attacks from any source. At that time, the President also had stated that "this program will be reviewed annually from the point of view of technical development, the evolving threat, and the diplomatic context including any talks on arms limitation," so as to "insure that we are doing as much as necessary but no more than that required by the threat existing at that time."

Participating in the review this year were the President's Foreign Intelligence Advisory Board, which made its own review of the threat, and the Department of Defense, including the Joint Chiefs of Staff, the President's Defense Program Review Committee, and the National Security Council, which reassessed alternative courses of action. This review showed that technical progress on all the components of the Safeguard system had been satisfactory. It also revealed that the threat had increased. The Soviet Union, bearing out predictions of last year, continued to construct intercontinental ballistic missiles and missile-carrying submarines at a steady pace, and continued a very active research and development program on new weapons. The Communist Chinese did not, so far as is known, test an ICBM during fiscal year 1970. However, by the summer of 1970 they appeared to be in a position to begin tests within a few months, having demonstrated the ability to put a satellite into orbit. It is simply a matter of time until they have an operational ICBM.

The annual review indicated that Strategic Arms Limitation Talks (SALT) were not jeopardized by approval of the first phase of Safeguard, and that until and unless an agreement is reached in SALT, the program should be continued. On the other hand, the United States intended to make the Nixon Doctrine foreign policy workable by providing adequate defenses to prevent other nations from engaging in diplomacy by nuclear blackmail in coming years.

The review also considered several alternatives, including canceling the Phase 1 Safeguard deployment approved last year or continuing Phase 1 only with additional research and development. However, in view of the continued growth of the Soviet threat and the prospect of Chinese deployment of an ICBM force in the mid-1970's, a year's delay in taking additional measures could not be justified.

The review also considered the effectiveness of the full twelve-site Safeguard system for the defense of Minuteman against a possible Soviet first strike, and options to counter such a threat effectively.

During this year, the Safeguard program proceeded with the initial congressionally approved increment (Phase 1) of two site complexes located in Minuteman fields near Grand Forks Air Force Base, North Dakota, and Malmstrom Air Force Base, Montana. The purposes of this Phase 1 deployment were to preserve the President's future options by establishing a minimum base for expansion if the need should arise; to work out the problems that inevitably arise in any new major weapon system; and to provide a beginning of protection for the Minuteman force against the mid-70's threat.

The research and development portion of the Safeguard program progressed satisfactorily. On Kwajalein Atoll in the Pacific, the prototype missile site radar (MSR) began radiating power in September 1968 and has been under checkout since that time. It met or bettered most of its design objectives and no serious deficiencies were found. MSR software for the first part of the system test program was completed and installed. Beginning in July 1969, tracking of local targets was accomplished, and in December 1969 two ICBM's launched from Vandenberg Air Force Base, California, were successfully tracked. Also at Kwajalein, the Spartan interceptor satisfactorily completed the first phase of development testing. There have been 15 launches, of which 11 were completely successful, 2 partially successful, and 2 failures. Two system tests with the Spartan integrated under MSR control have been conducted. One test was completely successful and the other only partially successful. The Sprint interceptor tests proceeded satisfactorily at White Sands Missile Range, New Mexico. Of 41 launches, 22 were completely successful, 9 partially successful, and 10 failures. Early problems were diagnosed and corrections confirmed by the last three successful flights. Plans called for an early conclusion of the White Sands tests and for system tests for Sprint to be started at Kwajalein.

The perimeter acquisition radar (PAR) was under fabrication, and the first installation was to be made at Grand Forks (the first

Safeguard operational site). No serious technical problems were encountered in this development, and there was confidence of meeting the schedule for the first PAR site. Certain important components were being tested as the year closed, and it was anticipated that by September 1970 about 95 percent of the PAR components would be released to production.

The task of integrating all of the major components into a system still lay ahead. Missile integration tests began during the year at Kwajalein, initially with the Spartan.

Command and control requirements for Safeguard joint operations with Air Force Minuteman missiles through interface at the CONAD-SAC level were defined. No problems were encountered.

Engineering design for the Grand Forks site was substantially completed and the contract was awarded. There was a delay of seven to nine months in the equipment readiness date of the Phase 1 sites, due in part to the delayed initiation of on-site activities pending congressional action on Phase 1 and in part to a need for a more economical and less compressed construction schedule.

In the year's Safeguard review, the developments in the threat that occurred in the last year since the administration decided to undertake Phase 1 were carefully evaluated. It was noted that Communist China continued to test nuclear devices which were expected to be suitable for ICBM application by the time their missile was developed. There was evidence that they continued to advance toward an ICBM capability, but the earliest date by which they could achieve this was considered to be in early 1973. This estimate represented about a one-year slippage. The Soviet buildup of SS9's deployed or believed to be under construction reached more than 300, as compared to about 230 in the spring of 1969. Development and testing of the 3-re-entry vehicle, SS9 configuration continued. The number of SS11's operational or under construction, estimated at about 700 last year, increased to more than 800. Soviet testing of the smaller SS11 ICBM suggested that certain improvements probably aimed at bettering the penetration capability were under development. And production of nuclear-powered, ballistic missile submarines continued at two Soviet shipyards, which together have a current construction rate of six to eight boats a year.

The administration's decision to request continuation of a phased Safeguard program for ballistic missile defense—going beyond the congressionally approved Phase 1—was based on several factors. Among them were careful consideration of the original objectives of Safeguard defense and of the need to maintain the President's flexibility on future options either to curtail or expand the system; the continued Chinese progress in nuclear weapons and the evolving and increasing Soviet offensive threat; the options currently available, considering technical progress and budgetary factors; the current international situation; the desire to continue emphasis on strategic defensive systems to assure the survivability of the deterrent force rather than being forced immediately to deploy additional offensive weapons; and the intent to maintain flexibility to adapt programs to any agreement which might result from successful arms limitation talks.

The deployment schedule, on the other hand, for the three sites contemplated (Grand Forks and Malmstrom, North Dakota, and Whiteman, Missouri) all fell within the late 1974–early 1975 time period. These were equipment readiness dates, on which equipment would be installed and operable, ready to be turned over to military control.

In February 1970, the Secretary of Defense asked the Congress for authorization to proceed with a modified Phase 2 Safeguard ballistic missile defense program, which was considered to be the minimum effort necessary both in cost and in deployment to fulfill the President's national security objectives.

The modified Phase 2 program for fiscal year 1971 requested congressional authorization for deployment of only one additional site near Whiteman Air Force Base, Missouri. It also recommended that authorization be given to undertake long lead-time advanced preparation work for five other sites without a deployment commitment: Northeast, Northwest, National Command Authority (Washington, D.C.), Warren Air Force Base in Wyoming, and the Michigan-Ohio area. The authorization request included advance purchase to make possible the eventual deployment of addition Sprint missiles at the original Phase 1 sites to further increase the defense of Minuteman.

The proposed program, although a minimum effort, maintained the President's options, after further review and decisions, to move, if necessary, toward a full Phase 2 twelve-site Safeguard defense, or to curtail the deployment if events or arms agreements dictated. Should they be needed, the full twelve sites could be installed by the late 1970's.

The twelve-site system would provide substantial protection for the U.S. population for a number of years against Communist Chinese or other third country attack, and adequate defense to allow most of the alert bomber force to take off even if subjected to surprise attack by submarine-launched missiles. Defense against an accidental launch from any source would also be provided by the twelve-site deployment. Further, as a prudent hedge against possible increased future threats to the U.S. deterrent, the proposed modified Phase 2 program would allow increases in Minuteman defense levels as the three sites in the Minuteman fields became operational.

In terms of program costs, the fiscal year 1971 budget submission included a request for $1.45 billion for Safeguard. This amount was necessary to continue Phase 1 deployment, to begin deployment at the one additional site, and to undertake advanced preparations at the five potential future sites. Actual expenditures during fiscal year 1971 for the Phase 2 increment of the program would be substantially less than $100 million.

The total DOD acquisition costs (including military construction, purchase of radars and missiles, and the cost of research, development, test and evaluation, but not operating costs) for the Phase 1 sites and the new Phase 2 sites at Whiteman—namely, for completing modified Phase 2—were estimated at $1.38 billion for fiscal year 1971, and a $5.9 billion total. The $5.9 billion acquisition cost, which would be authorized and appropriated over the period of fiscal years 1968–75, included development through system testing of the modified Spartan. Approximately $1.05 billion would be required in fiscal year 1971, if the program were restricted to Phase 1 only, with a total acquisition cost of $4.6 billion for Phase 1 only. Expenditures for fiscal year 1971, however, were specifically restricted to a minimum level as part of the administration's anti-inflationary efforts.

During the year, critics of Safeguard argued, as they had in the past, that the system would not give effective protection long enough to justify its costs. Questions were also raised about the suitability and measure of protection in defense of Minuteman against a possible Soviet first strike. Congressional attention focused on these and other issues about Safeguard's capabilities, particularly during the early part of the fiscal year. Finally, on August 6, 1969, after long debate in the Senate and throughout the country on the desirability of deploying the modified system, two amendments that would have prohibited spending on construction were defeated by razor-thin margins. As the year closed, the Army had approval to proceed with the limited Phase 1, while a vote on the proposal to proceed with a modified Phase 2 was still pending in Congress.

There were advances in various other weapons systems during the year. The quick reaction capability of the Pershing missile system was greatly improved with the development of new ground support equipment. The first battalion to receive the new equipment successfully completed annual service practice firings in September 1969, and all battalions in Europe were re-equipped by March 1970.

Deployment of the TOW antitank missile system to the training base in the continental United States was begun in the third quarter of the fiscal year. This weapon, which is tube-launched, optically tracked, and wire-guided, is designed for use by infantry and helicopter forces to destroy enemy tanks and other armored vehicles. It will upgrade the capability of U.S. forces to counter the armor threat that has existed in Europe since World War II.

Development of the Dragon guided missile system advanced during the year. This weapon is light enough to be carried and operated by one man and will give the foot soldier a lethal capability against enemy armor. Dragon will replace the 90-mm. recoilless rifle, which fails to meet the requirements for a medium antitank weapon in terms of range, portability, and kill probability.

In March 1970, following discussions with other nations in the North Atlantic Treaty Organization, the United States notified NATO headquarters that U.S. Army NATO forces would be equipped with the M16A1 rifle. Shipments were begun in May 1970 and were to be completed by September.

In August 1969 the Army accepted the M203 40-mm. grenade launcher attachment for the M16A1 rifle. The M203 replaces the M79, uses the same ammunition, and provides the grenadier with a weapon that is both a rifle and a grenade launcher. The M79 served only as a launcher and deprived the rifle squad of two rifles.

U.S. Army air defense forces were further reduced during the year by thirty-seven Nike-Hercules and sixteen Hawk firing batteries. All surface-to-air missiles were withdrawn from Vietnam and the total defenses in Hawaii and at Cincinnati-Dayton and Niagara-Buffalo were eliminated. Selected batteries were also inactivated in the area defenses of Detroit, Milwaukee, Philadelphia, Fort Bliss (Texas), Alaska, Germany, and Okinawa.

Some air defense battalions were reorganized, equipped, and trained as Hawk self-propelled units and several were deployed to Germany; one was retained at Fort Bliss, Texas. Some Chaparral and Vulcan batteries were activated during the year, and half were deployed overseas. This missile and gun combination provides defense against low altitude air attack.

Advanced development of the SAM-D surface-to-air missile system continued during the year. The Army has retained tight control over system specification, and plans the most austere design that is compatible with an efficient system to meet anticipated threats.

Army Aviation

During fiscal year 1970 an aviation structure for the Army in the post-Vietnam period was re-examined to incorporate the results of recent studies and to take advantage of Southeast Asia experience. A revised structure was developed that would make it possible to attain the most urgent airmobility objectives within established manning and dollar constraints. Resources for what were considered to be essential additions were provided for in part by trade-offs involving selected aviation and ground units. As over-all Army priorities were revised, some lesser priority aviation units were eliminated from the postwar structure in favor of new additions.

The revised structure improves force effectiveness by placing more aircraft and aviation units at key places; increases were obtained in divisional command and control aircraft, air cavalry units and aircraft, aerial firepower, and airmobile lift. The initial examination established priorities, guidelines, and procedures, which have since been applied to numerous alternative structures. In general, as the size of the total force decreases, proportionately more aviation support is both feasible and desirable, to provide additional firepower and mobility to the smaller force.

Several advances in aircraft safety have been introduced into Army aviation operations. Airborne proximity warning devices were installed at Fort Rucker, Alabama, for test and evaluation. These systems are designed to reduced the hazards of midair collision and the resultant loss of life and equipment. The ideal is to develop a system that would be adaptable to fleetwide use.

Development of an aircraft crash-resistant fuel system proceeded on schedule during the year. The first UH–1H production helicopter containing the new system was delivered to the Army on April 8, 1970. A program to install the system in older models will begin in July 1970. Development for the AH–1G and UH–1B/C helicopters was near completion at year's end, and development for other aircraft was proceeding. The program is scheduled to be completed by 1975.

There were developments in several Army aviation projects during fiscal year 1970. The OV–1D Mohawk, the latest version of the Army's medium observation aircraft, was introduced. It is a two-place, twin turboprop aircraft equipped with photographic and electronic sensors capable of monitoring enemy operations in daylight, dark, and inclement weather. The aircraft's external appearance is deceptively similar to the earlier versions, but a rapid modification capability enables a single OV–1D to perform the surveillance functions of any previous Mohawk. Three photographic systems can be installed or removed in less than an hour, and its radar and infrared systems are interchangeable. Thus the OV–1D can be quickly prepared to respond to a field commander's intelligence requirements. Several additional features were incorporated in this model to enhance its surveillance capabilities. It has an automatic data annotation system to identify all sensor imagery. There is a more accurate inertial navigation system as well as improved infrared and radar performance and displays. A vertical panoramic camera system photographs terrain from horizon to horizon. A radiological monitoring system is included, along with an aural recorder to transcribe crew descriptions of visual observations. And finally, there is electronic countermeasure equipment to provide greater assurance of mission success. In addition to this surveillance equipment, improvements have been made in areas of engine power, wing and landing gear strength, equipment accessibility, communications, and cockpit instrumentation.

The first CH–47C Chinook helicopter equipped with the new powerful T–55 and L–11 engines was deployed to operating units beginning in July 1969. This helicopter is the latest model of the Chinook fleet, capable of lifting a ten-ton payload, almost double that of the original model. This craft provides airmobility for military forces in the field, by transporting personnel, weapons, and cargo and providing rapid evacuation of wounded and recovery of downed aircraft.

The Army accepted delivery of the first CH–54B Tarhe helicopter in December 1969. The latest model of the Tarhe fleet, it provides improved performance and reliability, reduced maintenance, and a two-ton payload increase over older models. It is the Free World's largest flying crane helicopter and is capable of airlifting large bulk items of equipment (up to twelve tons), including artillery weapons, heavy engineer equipment, and downed aircraft.

And finally, delivery of OH–58 helicopters continued during the year. Produced under a five-year contract that calls for 2,200 aircraft by fiscal year 1972 and includes provisions to deal with escalation for inflation, the third year deliveries brought the total to 392 aircraft, of which 288 had been deployed to Southeast Asia as the year closed. The aircraft is performing well, meeting or surpassing Army expectations.

Chemical Warfare and Biological Research Programs

Presidential policy decisions, congressional legislation, and public opinion all had an unprecedented impact on the Army's chemical warfare and biological research programs during fiscal year 1970.

On November 25, 1969, the President announced a major change in national policy on chemical warfare and biological research; reaffirmed U.S. renunciation of first use of lethal chemical weapons in warfare; extended that renunciation to include incapacitating chemicals; confirmed that the United States would maintain a deterrent and a capability to retaliate with chemical agents if they are first used by an enemy against us; and banned all methods of biological warfare.

On February 14, 1970, the President renounced the use of toxins in warfare and directed the destruction of all such materials not required for research for defensive purposes. Concurrently, the term "biological warfare" (BW) was deleted as the designation of the biological research program.

The President also announced that the administration would submit the Geneva Protocol of 1925, which prohibits the first use of toxic chemical agents and bacteriological agents in war, to the Senate for advice and consent to ratification.

A week before his November policy statement, President Nixon had signed Public Law 91–121, which imposed far-reaching controls over the chemical warfare program. Under its provisions the Secretary of Defense must submit annual reports to Congress concerning funds spent for research, development, testing, evaluation, and procurement of chemical warfare agents. It also imposed controls on the testing and transportation of lethal chemical agents within the United States and on the testing, development, storage, and disposal of such agents outside the United States. It further prohibited the use of fiscal year 1970 appropriations for procurement of any delivery system specifically designed to disseminate any lethal agents, or any part or component of such a system, unless the President certified to Congress that such procurement was essential to the safety and security of the United States.

Because of public opinion and congressional protest, the Army deferred plans to dispose of obsolete chemical munitions and agents by dumping them in the Atlantic Ocean beyond the continental shelf. The National Academy of Sciences was asked to study the entire subject of disposal of chemical munitions. The academy recommended that mustard gas be destroyed by burning under strict pollution control, and that cluster bombs containing the nerve agent GB be disassembled and the agent chemically detoxified. By the close of the year, the Army had completed plans to dispose of these categories of munitions by the means proposed. In a more difficult case, the academy recommended that a panel of specialists study methods for disposing of another type of stockpiled materiel—rockets filled with a nerve agent and encased in concrete coffins as a safety measure until disposal. As the year closed, the study committee had suggested several ways of disposing of these items, and a decision was pending. (For additional details of the effects of the new policy on the Army's research and development program and the shipment of hazardous materials, see chapters 9 and 11.)

V. Personnel

Military Personnel

Army strength decreased substantially during fiscal year 1970, from 1,512,169 to 1,322,548. The drop reflected the inactivation of 2⅓ divisions withdrawn from Vietnam and a lower trainee population at the close of the year. The end-of-year strength included 166,721 officers, 1,153,013 enlisted personnel, and 2,814 cadets. (Strength figures include reimbursable personnel except where otherwise indicated. Reimbursable personnel are those performing duty with other government agencies and for whose services the Army receives reimbursement from the using agency.) There were about 39,500 officer accessions during the year, and closing strength in this category showed the first decrease since 1963. A total of 198,700 men were inducted into the Army, and 177,300 men and women enlisted for the first time. Compared with fiscal year 1969, these figures represented a decrease of about 56,000 inductions and 23,600 first enlistments.

In Vietnam, Army strength dropped for the first time since the start of the American buildup there. Operating strength decreased from about 361,000 to around 299,000 as the fiscal year closed. Three redeployments totaling 58,789 Army military personnel were completed during the year, and plans were made for a fourth to be completed in October 1970.

ACCESSION OF OFFICERS BY SOURCE IN FISCAL YEAR 1970	
Source	
Service academies	707
Reserve Officers' Training Corps	15,803
Officer Candidate School	8,970
Voluntary active duty	2,358
Professional (JAG, WAC, MSC, CHAP)	929
Medical Corps, Dental Corps, Veterinary Corps	3,132
Regular Army appointments (from civil life)	26
Miscellaneous [a]	588
Nurses and medical specialists	1,488
Warrant officers	5,502
Total [b]	39,503

[a] Includes administrative gains such as recall from retired list and interservice transfer (includes 250 unidentified accessions).
[b] Excludes reimbursable personnel.

The assignment of top quality officers to adviser duty in Vietnam became increasingly important as the Vietnamization program expanded. To the Province Senior Adviser Program, already established, was added a District Senior Adviser Program. Both are considered key assignments requiring careful personnel nomination and selection. Tour lengths are twelve months with a six-month extension option for deserving officers. Various incentives are offered, including special considerations concerning leave, duty assignment, subsequent duty preference, schooling, family housing, and special pay. As the year closed an intelligence adviser program was being developed.

The total number of warrant officers decreased from 23,729 to 23,007 during the year. About 49 percent of authorized warrant officer positions were in Army aviation specialties. Over 1,700 warrant officers who demonstrated exceptional abilities and potential were awarded direct commissions.

Over 177,000 men and women entered the Army on first enlistments in fiscal year 1970. Although this was less than in 1969, it still represented a larger proportion of total nonprior-service gains— 47 percent as compared to the 45 percent achieved last year.

Project 100,000, the program under which the Army accepts 12 percent of its new recruits from those previously disqualified for service because of mental or physical deficiencies, continued to function as a part of the over-all enlisted procurement program. Another effort, the intensified recruitment program, was concentrated on obtaining men from areas of high unemployment. Over 7,900 men were enlisted from designated poverty areas in forty-three major cities and the Navajo Indian Reservation.

Two new enlisted options were established to attract men and women to an Army career. Designed to take advantage of civilian-acquired skills and based on a recognition of the fact that all enlisted personnel need not enter at the bottom, the options seek to attract individuals with medical or construction skills qualifying them for rapid advancement to grades E–4 or E–5. Men with three years of experience in the building trades, for example, are appointed to E–5 upon completion of basic combat training and assigned to the construction foreman skill development base course for supervisory training.

Moreover, since two-year college-level technical and vocational schools offer a valuable source of technically trained personnel, military occupational specialties were being reviewed to see which ones could be awarded directly to graduates of these schools. A pilot procurement program along this line should be operational by the fall of 1971.

General public dissatisfaction with alleged inequities in the Selective Service System generated several draft reforms during the year. Following the enactment of Public Law 91–124, which amended the Military Selective Service Act of 1967, Executive Order Number 11497, issued on November 26, 1969, directed that a random selection system (lottery draft) be established. A national drawing was held in Washington, D.C., on December 1, 1969. Under the new system, put into effect on January 1, 1970, the random selection sequence determined the order of selection for military training and service of all eligible registrants who were between nineteen and twenty-six years old on January 1, 1970. On April 23, 1970, Executive Order No. 11527 announced additional reforms to make the system more equitable by ending all future occupational and paternity deferments, except in cases of genuine hardship. Concurrently, a presidential message to Congress requested legislative authority to phase out student deferments except for officer training programs such as ROTC, and to establish draft calls on the basis of a national sequence of numbers.

These reforms increased the size of the eligible manpower pool, sought to equalize induction liability, and blunted some of the criticisms of the selection process.

The elimination of occupational deferments will result in the loss to the civilian economy of some personnel with usable civilian skills, and the number of junior enlisted personnel with dependents can be expected to increase with the ending of future paternity deferments. The abolition of future student deferments proposed by the President will have a major impact on the Army, especially in the area of officer procurement. The proposal to establish draft calls on the basis of a national sequence of numbers will have little effect on the Army other than possibly to improve the attitude of draftees as a result of the more equitable selection procedures.

The presidential commission studying the subject of an all-volunteer armed force concluded that it is both feasible and desirable. To achieve this ultimate goal, the Army created a task group to study, develop, co-ordinate, and monitor actions designed to reduce reliance on the draft. These efforts are expected to increase the attractiveness of the service and move the Army toward an all-volunteer force.

Work was under way to implement approved actions which do not require legislation or increased funding. Others await further study, funds, or legislative authority.

A significant number of college graduates were inducted into the Army following the termination of graduate deferments. The Army made every effort to assign them to activities that made use of their prior training, education, experience, and leadership potential, to the benefit of both the individual and the military service. A survey of Army positions and occupational specialties identified three categories of skill against which college graduates could be considered: priority I embraces skills that can be correlated to academic fields or personal preferences of college graduates, such as officer training, scientific or engineering fields, or language training; priority II consists of skills that challenge the leadership or technical capabilities of college men, such as combat arms potential, radar technology, or automatic data processing. Priority III comprises skills that are essential but do not challenge or make use of the background of the average college graduate, for example, driver, cook, or shoe repairman. Of the 32,280 college graduates inducted in fiscal year 1970, 19,676 (61 percent) were given assignments in priority I, 12,604 (39 percent) in priority II, and none in priority III.

Nearly 187,000 men have been accepted by the Army under Project 100,000, the enlisted procurement program. Thirty percent of the men had a reading ability below fifth grade level and had to have remedial reading instruction to help them qualify in basic and advanced training. Otherwise, these men were trained in courses at regular training centers and schools. They were trained and assigned in about 145 military occupational specialties, about 125 of which are related to civilian-type skills and trades. As the year closed, 41 percent were assigned to combat skills and 59 percent in support skills. Over 95 percent of the men accepted under this program are performing adequately in their jobs.

In addition to programs like Project 100,000, which are designed to prepare individuals to be better soldiers, the Army has administered several programs to help military personnel make a smooth transition back to civilian life, taking with them some skills that would assure them a reasonable opportunity for employment. Project Transition has afforded many Army personnel the opportunity to sort out and take advantage of occupational options within the service that could be applied upon return to civilian life. In the past fiscal year this program, involving counseling, skill and educational training, and job placement information, operated at 55 installations in the continental United States. Some 114,000 separating soldiers have taken advantage of Project Transition training since the program's inception in 1968, and 5,000 were participating in the closing month of fiscal year 1970.

On June 1, 1970, a Department of Defense referral program began operation. It is designed to enhance the employment opportunities of the 65,000 to 70,000 servicemen who retire from the armed forces annually after serving twenty to thirty years in uniform. The Army has made this a part of its unfunded retirement services program. To the extent that resources allow, this service assists retirees in their move to a second career. It improves communication between them and prospective employers, and complements retention programs by providing desirable services to those who elect a full career.

In line with a continuing effort to simplify the procedures of the Army Personnel Information System, a new technique to automate source data was developed and field tested during the fall of 1969. Called Mark Sense Data Automation, it employs mark sense forms and optical mark readers to capture and reduce data to computer-usable form. The test confirmed the accuracy, timeliness, and cost-effectiveness of the technique, and it was approved for Army-wide application in the Military Personnel Information System beginning in fiscal year 1971.

In November 1969 a centralized transient account system was established under which the responsibility of accounting for transients was transferred from units and data processing activities at major command and Army levels to Headquarters, Department of the Army. Under the new procedure, personnel accounting procedures are correlated with the physical presence of the individual. Personnel departing on a permanent change of station are dropped from the losing unit's morning report on the day of departure, and are not added to the gaining unit's morning report strength until the reporting date specified in the reassignment orders or the date of physical arrival, whichever occurs first. Thus units are no longer accountable for an extended period after an individual departs or for any period prior to his arrival.

Although the Army has led the nation in providing and insuring equality of opportunity and treatment for all personnel, recent events in the military services, coupled with unrest in civilian communities and educational institutions, demonstrated the need for a comprehensive reassessment of the Army's Equal Opportunity and Treatment of Military Personnel Program. A broad assessment was conducted by the Army Staff and the program was expanded and intensified. Briefings on racial tension in the Army were presented to commanders in Europe, the Pacific, and the Canal Zone, as well as to general officers and key staff members in the departmental headquarters and the Continental Army Command. Personnel of all grades and races participated in equal opportunity and racial tension seminars at numerous headquarters and installations during December 1969 and January 1970, culminating in a seminar at the Continental Army Command headquarters in February 1970. This command was directed to develop a course of instruction in race relations for presentation at training centers and service schools beginning in fiscal year 1971. The instruction is designed to develop among all personnel an understanding of the basic factors in race relations, the causes of tension, and steps to foster harmony among all personnel.

The Secretary of the Army in a speech before the Association of the United States Army in October 1969 identified some areas of concern and some of the measures that would get at the roots of the problem. Among them was the need to emphasize the personal responsibility of each leader for racial harmony among his men; to improve communication on racial matters; to understand the Negro soldier's interests and recognize his contributions to the Army; to improve Army-community relations; to advance interpersonal relations through training programs and service school courses; and to improve the prospects for minority group personnel when they complete military service.

Numerous other measures were undertaken throughout the Army to correct inequalities and improve relations. The variety of merchandise stocked in post exchanges and the literature carried in libraries and on newsstands were expanded to encompass the needs and tastes of members of minority groups. Along this line, attention was given to the type and variety of entertainment offered in clubs, and the portrayal of minority group personnel and their achievements in publications and films. Recruitment of minority group junior officers was also emphasized.

The results of these Army-wide efforts were encouraging. Yet personnel turnover, with an influx of socially conscious youths, creates a continuing challenge in a complex situation, and much may be done in the military to improve racial harmony and continue to set an example for other segments of American society.

Housing is as important to the morale and welfare of military personnel as the equal opportunity, educational, and counseling programs outlined above. Based on long-range strength and deployment estimates, the Army needs 355,743 family housing units. With available assets of 218,756 units on and off post, a sizable deficit exists. Allowing for program safety factors, the deficit totals 63,800 units. Only 1,700 units will be funded under the fiscal year 1971 program, and such a small annual increment does not permit significant progress in reducing the deficit or promise sufficient housing to accommodate the proposed all-volunteer Army.

There is also a substantial deficit in bachelor housing for officers and enlisted men around the world. Army personnel are still housed in obsolete World War II buildings at many locations. About 32,000 new bachelor officer quarters spaces and 230,000 enlisted men's barracks spaces are needed. Deficits at permanent installations in the continental United States, Alaska, Hawaii, and the Canal Zone amount to about 13,000 spaces for officers and 123,000 enlisted barracks spaces. To overcome the backlog, annual outlays of $100 million for barracks and $50 million for bachelor officers' quarters would be required over the next ten years.

Military Justice, Discipline, and Legal Affairs

The Military Justice Act of 1968 became fully effective on August 1, 1969. Changes in the Uniform Code of Military Justice improved both the efficiency and fairness of the military judicial system. Additional Judge Advocate General's Corps officers needed to provide for requirements under the act were at their duty stations by the close of the year. The use of lawyer counsel and military judges has significantly improved trials by special courts-martial. Military judges are being detailed to approximately 85 percent of the special courts-martial in the Army, and it is anticipated that this figure will increase. The provision for trial by the military judge alone is being used extensively at both special and general courts-martial. About 95 percent of the special courts-martial to which military judges are detailed and 86 percent of the general courts-martial are being tried by the military judge alone at the accused's request. The use of the provision has decreased trial time, shortened trial records, and resulted in a significant saving of line officer time. Other procedural innovations in the act have been particularly beneficial in complicated cases, such as those arising out of the Son My incident (see chapter 3).

There were 58,999 persons tried by court-martial during fiscal year 1970, a rate of 40.05 per 1,000 as compared with 76,320 in fiscal year 1969, a rate of 49.92 per 1,000. The following table compares totals and rates per thousand by type for fiscal years 1969 and 1970.

Type	1969 Total	1969 Rate per 1,000	1970 Total	1970 Rate per 1,000
General court-martial	2,482	1.62	2,628	1.78
Special court-martial	59,597	38.98	41,348	28.07
Summary court-martial	14,421	9.32	15,023	10.20

In addition to these courts-martial proceedings, 318,200 persons were punished under the provisions of Article 15 of the Uniform

Code of Military Justice (216.0 per 1,000) as compared with 301,095 in fiscal year 1969 (196.0 per 1,000).

Under Article 86 of the code, 1,349 individuals were convicted by general courts-martial for absence without leave (AWOL), as compared with 1,158 in the previous year. Under Article 85 of the code, 185 individuals were convicted by general courts-martial for desertion, as compared with 140 in fiscal year 1969. Under special courts-martial proceedings, bad conduct discharges were given to 464 individuals for absence without leave and to 1 for desertion.

Command attention was placed on the AWOL and desertion problems, and seminars were conducted at installation, Army, and Continental Army Command headquarters, which proved to be of great assistance to junior officers and noncommissioned officers, the leaders in the best position to influence potential offenders.

Since early 1968, disciplinary problems have been on the rise in the Army, with increased absenteeism, use of drugs, antiwar agitation, racial tensions, and resistance to discipline. While much of this rise has been a reflection of changing national attitudes and reflects social problems in the civilian society, the threat to morale and discipline in the Army has been a matter of grave military concern.

Dissent in the Army has taken various forms, ranging from the usual gripes of soldiers to individual participation in coffeehouse activities, publication and distribution of underground literature, participation in antiwar meetings and demonstrations, and involvement in other forms of protest. The Army has monitored such activity for two years. A leveling trend in the number of known and suspected dissidents in the Army began in December 1969, and over the course of fiscal year 1970 there was a downward trend in the number of incidents related to dissent. While there is no evidence that these activities have adversely affected the Army's combat effectiveness, the potential for undermining discipline and lowering morale more than justifies continuing attention to the problems in this area.

In September 1969 the permanent subcommittee on investigations of the U.S. Senate's Committee on Government Operations conducted investigations and hearings on fraud and corruption in the management of military club systems, and of illegal currency manipulations affecting the Republic of Vietnam. The hearings disclosed substantial irregularities and deficiencies in the operation of Army noncommissioned officers' open messes in Europe, the Republic of Vietnam, and the United States. The Army launched a major investigation and a number of active and former commissioned and noncommissioned officers were named and called as witnesses. The Assistant Secretary of Defense for Manpower and Reserve Affairs was the initial witness in the congressional hearings, and the Secretary of the Army testified in March 1970 concerning Army actions to eliminate and preclude recurrences of the alleged irregularities, including tighter management and control over the operation of clubs and open messes. Proceedings were continuing as the year closed.

There were several developments under the Army Correction Program during the year. To improve the Army stockade system, over 2,000 correctional specialists were trained, authorizations were approved for the assignment of more than 1,400 additional personnel to stockade staffs, and over $8 million in new stockade construction—based on modern correctional concepts and designs—was authorized at four military installations.

The special civilian committee for the study of the U.S. Army's confinement system, composed of six prominent civilian penologists appointed by the Secretary of the Army in April 1969, published its final report in June 1970. The committee recognized the Army's concern for operating confinement facilities in an enlightened and humane manner. While finding numerous examples of superb leadership and dedication at all levels, it found that the Army falls short of its goals in many respects. To deal with the broad, complex, and delicate problems that exist in the Army's correction program, the committee recommended substantial organizational changes, and actions to modernize the program were initiated during the fiscal year.

There were 21,278 cases during the year ending November 30, 1969, in which U.S. Army personnel overseas were charged with offenses that were subject to the jurisdiction of foreign courts. In 8,725 of these cases, the offenses charged were solely violations of foreign law and thus subject to the jurisdiction of foreign courts. The remaining 12,553 cases involved alleged violations of both U.S. military law and foreign law, over which the foreign country had the primary right to exercise jurisdiction. Foreign authorities waived their primary right in 11,550, or 92 percent, of these cases. Of the 6,766 U.S. personnel finally tried by foreign courts, only 109 received sentences to confinement that were not suspended.

During fiscal year 1970, the U.S. Army Claims Service monitored Army claims obligations worldwide; 75,924 claims against the U.S. government were processed, with $19,754,866.85 paid in settlement. The claims service also recovered $1,842,483.67 from carriers, warehousemen, insurers, and other third parties.

The Department of Defense, as well as other executive agencies of the U.S. government, is a major user of commercial communications facilities, and contracts for package services at bulk rates. Bell System companies and the Western Union Telegraph Company are major suppliers of these services, and the bulk facilities and rates pricing arrangement of these companies is identified in the TELPAK pricing arrangement. Pricing by groups of circuits rather than by individual channels means substantial savings to a user, and the Defense Department and other executive agencies purchase well over $100 million a year in TELPAK services.

On October 1, 1969, the American Telephone and Telegraph Company filed proposed rate increases for TELPAK services with the Federal Communications Commission (FCC), requesting that they become effective on November 1, 1969. The proposed increase would raise the cost of services to the federal government by more than $44 million annually.

The Regulatory Law Division of the Office of the Judge Advocate General, by appropriate delegations of authority from the administrator of the General Services Administration and the Secretary of Defense, was designated to represent all federal executive agencies in such proceedings as might be appropriate before the Federal Communications Commission in connection with the proposed TELPAK increases. The Regulatory Law Division filed two petitions protesting the rate increase, one on October 16, 1969, to reject or require withdrawal of the proposed increases, the other on October 16, 1969, for investigation and suspension and for an accounting order. The FCC, in a decision released on November 6, 1969, granted the petition for investigation and suspension and for an accounting order which delayed the effective date of the TELPAK increase until February 1, 1970—a delay that saved the Department of Defense and the executive agencies over $11 million. Beginning on the latter date, these agencies, including Defense, began paying the increased rates, subject to refund should the charges in question be found unjustified. As the year closed, the Judge Advocate General's Regulatory Law Division was preparing the government's case in litigation that is expected to last for up to two years.

Health and Medical Care

The rate of admission for Army active duty personnel to hospitals and quarters during fiscal year 1970 was 346 per 1,000 average strength per year, slightly lower than the 376 per 1,000 in 1969. The noneffective rate, representing the average daily number of

Army active duty personnel in an excused-from-duty status due to medical causes per 1,000 average strength, declined to 17.6 from 19.4 in the prior year. Noneffectiveness due to injuries resulting from hostile actions declined to 4.2 from 5.4 in 1969.

The following table displays admission rates in Vietnam and other areas, for disease and injuries as well as for other causes, and includes the incidence rates of malaria and certain other conditions which may cause a high proportion of noneffectiveness in one or more of the areas.

ADMISSIONS TO HOSPITALS AND QUARTERS AND INCIDENCE OF SELECTED CONDITIONS—U.S. ARMY PERSONNEL ON ACTIVE DUTY FISCAL YEAR 1970

(Rates per 1,000 average strength per year)

	World-wide	CONUS Army Areas	Oversea Areas Total	Europe	Pacific All Areas	Pacific Vietnam
Admissions						
All causes	346	354	336	210	394	442
Disease	290	321	257	179	290	314
Injury	56	33	79	31	104	128
Incidence [a]						
Malaria	7.19	3.04	11.58	0.29	16.83	18.49
Diarrheal diseases	20.20	14.59	26.13	12.90	30.73	34.47
Acute upper respiratory infection and influenza	94.32	149.82	35.55	39.01	30.81	29.20
Skin diseases Dermatophytosis	9.52	5.32	13.98	2.34	19.70	22.83
Neuropsychiatric conditions	14.04	11.86	16.35	9.63	19.55	20.94
Hepatitis Viral	3.38	2.48	4.34	0.40	6.35	6.54

[a] Includes Army personnel wounded or injured as a result of actions of hostile forces.

The Military Blood Program Agency continued to co-ordinate the service's blood programs that support operational commanders. Since June 1966, over 875,000 units of whole blood have been shipped to Southeast Asia. The Army operates seventeen donor centers strategically situated near large troop concentrations, and has provided over 50 percent of the blood furnished for that area. The use of whole blood in replacement therapy is emphasized in medical care in Southeast Asia and is facilitated by rapid evacuation of the wounded to well-equipped hospitals. There is no shortage of blood for transfusions in Vietnam. Requirements have been met without assistance from nonmilitary resources. Blood is obtained from military personnel, their dependents, and Department of Defense personnel at military installations.

Advances under the program were made in the use of component therapy, involving the process of separating blood into its different cellular and protein components—red cells, white cells, platelets, antihemophilic factor, albumin, fibrinogen, and gamma globulin. In this way, the blood of one donor can help up to seven patients by providing only the component needed. More use of component therapy will not only reduce waste but be safer and more effective for the patient.

During the year a major study of the Army Medical Department was conducted to determine what organizational modifications might be adopted to make the Army's worldwide medical support more effective. The study group, chaired by the Deputy Surgeon General and staffed by Army military and civilian personnel, analyzed the functional areas that have an impact, however slight, upon the Medical Department's mission and the Surgeon General's command and staff responsibilities; assessed the worldwide performance of the Medical Department under its existing organization; inquired into trends in health care, resource management, medical information system development, and the organization of health services within and outside of the military; and developed and evaluated alternative organizational structures. Analyzed were such functional areas as manpower, personnel, materiel, and financial management; the operation of medical treatment facilities and joint agencies; combat developments; information systems; facilities design and construction; medical intelligence; patient evacuation; preventive medicine; medical research and development; force development; and medical planning. These analyses dealt with the present medical planning, programing, and budgeting system as it related to Medical Department objectives, to organizational structure and operating procedures, to communications and information, to studies in progress, and to the constraints and problems that influence the Surgeon General's broad responsibility for managing the Army's health services. As the year closed the report was being co-ordinated with major Army commands and the Army Staff, preparatory to submission to the Chief of Staff in July 1970.

Civilian Personnel

The Department of the Army uses civilians where it is more economical to do so and where military occupancy of a position is not required for training or rotational purposes. Substantial economies are achieved by using civilians in many professional, administrative, technical, and clerical positions.

Civilian personnel strength declined by 9 percent in fiscal year 1969, from 577,045 on June 30, 1969, to 521,796 on June 30, 1970. The reduction in U.S. citizens was also 9 percent. The largest personnel cut occurred in Southeast Asia where the number of local nationals fell by about 9,000 employees to approximately 34,000, a decline of 21 percent. There was also a substantial cut of about 19 percent of indigenous employees in Japan.

The department's equal employment opportunity program received continued emphasis. The Secretary of the Army and the Chief of Staff jointly sponsored the Command Equal Employment Opportunity Institute in Washington, D.C., in March 1970. This institute was followed by nine regional seminars to stimulate and promote the program throughout the department.

Equally important was the publication of a departmental plan of action containing the latest Civil Service Commission, Department of Defense, and Department of the Army policies on equal employment opportunity and listing actions to correct existing problems; commands and installations used this master document to develop plans tailored to their levels.

A variety of special employment plans were emphasized during the year: the President's Stay-In-School Campaign, Project Value, Project Hire, summer employment of youth, Veteran's Readjustment Appointment Program, and employment of the handicapped. Substantial progress was made in many of these programs. Project Hire was established to promote the hiring of Alaskan natives (Eskimos and Aleut Indians) in their home state; the Veterans Readjustment Appointment Program was implemented during the year; and the Secretary of the Army issued a statement on employment of the handicapped and the second annual Handicapped Employee of the Year award was made. But despite over-all success, some difficulties were encountered with these special programs. Project Value, designed to train disadvantaged youths for permanent jobs, was completed but was only partially successful in providing permanent Department of Defense employees. Reductions in funds and spaces had an adverse effect upon some of the special programs.

The new federal promotion and internal placement policy, and the accompanying Army program, was installed at all activities on January 1, 1970. In accordance with an extension of the mandatory implementation date granted by the Civil Service Commission, a number of activities used the last six months of 1969 to test and modify their programs before installing them on a permanent basis. In addition to issuing policies, regulations, and other guidance, the Department of the Army assisted field activities in making their transition to the new program, holding five regional workshops at central locations around the country. These workshops were attended by those responsible for installation recruitment and placement programs.

As the evaluation of employees is the most important aspect of the placement program, the Army suggested that a Department of Defense applicant evaluation committee be established. As the year closed, this committee was developing applicant evaluation programs such as the job qualification system for trades and labor occupations, to be installed by all federal agencies for wage grade positions by January 1, 1971.

The recruitment during the year of 285 U.S. citizens for positions in Vietnam met most of the needs in that area. In accordance with Army policy, nearly all were recruited from among Army civilian employees in the United States. Authorized civilian strength for U.S. Army, Vietnam, was reduced from 787 to 706 during this period. Many recruitment requests were canceled and others were suspended while internal adjustments were made to reach the new strength ceiling. Another fifty-six nonappropriated fund employees, primarily librarians and recreational specialists, departed for Vietnam assignments during the year and twenty-three other employees were selected to fill spaces early in fiscal year 1971.

In the field of career management, progress was made toward the achievement of long-range goals. Six nationwide conferences were held to interpret to field administrators the guidance published late last year on improving the management of career records and to stimulate field interest in this unspectacular but important aspect of the program. Basic policies and requirements for the various career fields were updated and revised.

An improved statistical report led to refinements in reporting career management activities and materially assisted the Army in monitoring the progress of career interns. The fiscal year witnessed greater strides in the involvement of the functional chiefs in their various career programs. This greater involvement led to an improved selection process and contributed to reducing the time required to issue Army-wide referral lists to ten days or less in many cases.

The most important step forward was the identification of 4,000 civilian positions in career occupations to be filled at the entrance level in fiscal year 1970. Because of cuts in funds and civilian spaces, the full extent of which had not been foreseen when the goal was established, the objective was not reached. The final total of career interns hired in fiscal year 1970 was about 2,100, slightly over half of the initial objective. Despite severe budgetary restrictions, an input of talented young people with potential for filling the Army's key jobs in the future has been maintained.

The Army continued to work with the Civil Service Commission and the Office of the Secretary of Defense to develop grade structure and evaluation plans, regulations, and instructions for the Coordinated Federal Wage System. As the year closed, conversion of Army wage board employees to this new governmentwide system was proceeding according to plan as locality wage schedules, resulting from surveys, became effective. Full-scale wage surveys will be completed and all wage areas converted by November 1970.

The major event in labor relations during the year was President Nixon's issuance of Executive Order 11491, Labor-Management Relations in the Federal Service, on October 29, 1969. The new executive order provided a complete restructuring of the federal labor relations program, and the Department of the Army conducted an intensive Army-wide program to familiarize key managers with its provisions. Twenty orientation workshops were held during the last half of the year: eleven in the continental United States, two in U.S. Army, Pacific, and seven in U.S. Army, Europe. Over 1,000 military and civilian managers attended these seminars and were provided training packages to use in conducting their own orientation for subordinate managers and supervisors.

Representatives of the Department of the Army worked closely with the Office of the Assistant Secretary of Defense (Manpower and Reserve Affairs) in developing Defense-wide guidance on the new executive order. The limited additional guidance needed for the department's field installations was issued as a civilian personnel regulation. Once the regulation was issued, attention was directed to revising Department of the Army training courses and pamphlets on labor relations.

There was continued growth in the scope of labor relations activity within the Army during fiscal year 1970. The number of exclusive bargaining units increased from 461 in June 1969 to 515 at the end of June 1970. The number of employees in these 54 new units totaled 14,415, but because of the reduction in force conducted during the year, the net increase in the number of employees covered by exclusive recognition was only 3,000 (from 157,000 to 160,000). The number of approved agreements with labor unions rose by 30, to 273, during the same period.

The suggestions of civilian employees and military personnel continue to be an important factor in increasing efficiency and reducing the cost of operating the department. During fiscal year 1970, civilian employees submitted 77,697 suggestions, 24,286 of which were adopted. First year benefits from the adopted suggestions amounted to $74.6 million dollars. This figure is slightly lower than last year because of the turbulence created by installation closings and reductions in force. Military personnel submitted 54,656 suggestions, 5,612 of which were adopted. First year benefits from these suggestions were $47.1 million. This is a substantial gain over fiscal year 1969 and demonstrates the success which the department has had in extending the suggestion program, for many years limited to civilians, to its military personnel.

Since fiscal 1966, the Department of the Army has vigorously fostered a program of long-term training and education of key civilian employees. The primary purpose of the program is to help assure that the department keeps abreast of managerial, technical, and scientific advancements, both in and out of the federal government. That the training contributes substantially to employee effectiveness has been shown by periodic formal evaluations by top managers of the installations, the immediate supervisors of the trainees, and individual trainees who have returned to their jobs.

The functional chiefs of the various occupations and disciplines and the local training committees have been very helpful in the process of selecting employees for long-term training. Through their efforts, attention is given to such matters as potential benefits to the organization, timeliness and appropriateness of proposed education to the career development of the employee, and balance and fairness in helping to assure that deserving employees in some segments are not overlooked while others get a disproportionate share of the opportunities.

Long-term training is aimed at anticipated future needs of the department as well as current requirements. Despite economy measures, which are being extensively applied, commanders have been urged to make every effort to continue support of the long-term training and education program. To supplement their efforts, a substantial pool of funds and manpower spaces is maintained centrally.

In April 1970, the Army Civilian Training Center moved into new quarters in the Forrestal Building in Washington, D.C., equipped with an auditorium, seminar rooms, and publication facilities.

The Army Civilian Training Center manages the Army's worldwide program of personnel management for executives training and conducts this course for Army executives in the Washington, D.C., Virginia, and Maryland area. It also develops and conducts other Army civilian training courses and provides a joint-use training facility for other federal agencies.

VI. Reserve Forces

Organized into eight combat divisions and twenty-one combat brigades, the Army Reserve Components are the initial and primary source of the additional units and individuals required to reinforce and support deployed active Army forces and the Strategic Reserve when a mobilization occurs. Consisting of the Army National Guard and the Army Reserve, the components provide forces needed to expand the training and support base in emergencies. Support units are included to round out active Army forces and provide the necessary balance in the Reserve Components.

The Army Staff develops contingency plans that govern the structure and the priorities assigned to the Reserve Components. This program currently reflects the exigencies of brush fire wars of recent experience at the expense of planning for general war. In 1968 a reorganization eliminated a number of units and concentrated their resources in units specifically cited in these contingency plans. In the interest of ·bringing all Army National Guard (ARNG) and Army Reserve (USAR) forces to roughly equal levels of readiness, the Department of the Army in September 1969 dropped the priority system prevalent under the selected reserve force (SRF) concept and incorporated the Reserve Components structure into the Department of the Army's master priority list.

The fiscal year also saw the release from active duty of all units that had been mobilized in May 1968. Of seventy-six Army National Guard and Army Reserve units mobilized, forty-three served in Vietnam. The last of the forty-three units was released from active duty on November 26, 1969. The remaining thirty-three, which were assigned to the U.S. Strategic Army Forces (STRAF), were released by December 12, 1969. A total of 19,874 Army National Guardsmen and Reservists were mobilized, 17,415 as members of units and 2,459 as individuals from the Individual Ready Reserve.

Readiness

The readiness of the Reserve Components improved during the year, although at a less than acceptable rate because of the lack of adequate modern equipment, the shortage of tactical training areas near home stations, and a paucity of qualified personnel. Among efforts to resolve some of these problems was a test program which should determine the maximum readiness feasible before mobilization.

Since the primary concern of the reserve force is to respond quickly to a call for mobilization and make units available to the active Army as speedily as possible, the Department of the Army also initiated late in the fiscal year a series of ten projects to investigate the maximum level of preparedness under austere budget conditions. The study was continuing as the year closed.

Personnel

A detailed study of officer personnel policy conducted in 1968 produced several recommendations for improving the management of the Reserve Components' officer corps. By 1969 many of these recommendations had been introduced and were fully effective; others were to be incorporated gradually to insure equitable treatment of officers of long standing in the reserve forces and those of more recent membership. A few of the recommendations required additional study or the enactment of legislation before they could become part of the procedure designed to produce, promote, and retain highly qualified reserve officers.

The Army has recognized the need for equity between the enlisted reservist called to active duty and the inductee or regular Army dischargee who has a remaining reserve obligation. Enlisted reservists who were ordered to active duty in the 1968 mobilization and who served in Vietnam or had at least two years of active duty, including active duty for training, were authorized to apply for transfer to the Individual Ready Reserve for the remainder of their statutory obligation. The applications of Army National Guardsmen remained subject to the approval of state governors.

To provide adequate active duty training for individuals entering the Reserve Enlistment Program (REP), the Army allotted part of the Army training base, including every military occupational skill category, to the Reserve Components. This move reduced the time between enlistment and the beginning of training to an acceptable level, except in a few special skill areas or for training that requires a security clearance.

The fiscal year 1970 Defense Authorization Act prescribed an average paid drill strength of not less than 393,298 in units of the ARNG and 255,591 in units of the USAR. This strength permits Reserve Component units to be manned at over 90 percent of wartime (TOE) strength. The following table depicts the status of the paid drill strength of the Reserve Components as of June 30, 1970.

	ARNG	USAR	Total
TOE	438,300	272,700	711,000
Authorized average	393,298	255,591	648,889
Actual average	392,388	257,490	649,878

Enlisted accessions in Reserve Component units during fiscal year 1970 are shown in the following table.

	ARNG	USAR	Total
Nonprior service	104,464	44,459	148,923
Prior service	14,725	9,643	24,368 [a]
Total	119,189	54,102	173,291

[a] Does not include 3,179 ARNG and 5,310 USAR re-enlistments.

The following table depicts the individual training status of both components at the end of the fiscal year.

	ARNG	USAR	Total
Assigned strengths	409,192	260,654	669,846
REP awaiting training	34,941	17,281	52,222
REP in training	42,508	20,167	62,675
REP training completed in fiscal year	53,454	46,607	100,061
Trained strength	331,743	223,206	554,949
Percent of assigned trained	81.1	86.0	83.0

The following table depicts the status of technicians in the Reserve Components as of June 30, 1970.

	ARNG	USAR	Total
Required	26,519	6,838	33,357
Authorized	24,328	6,127	30,455
Percent of required assigned	89.5	87.8	89.1
Percent of authorized assigned	97.5	98.0	97.6

The number of active Army advisers assigned to the Reserve Components as of June 30, 1970, is given in the following table.

	ARNG	USAR	Total
Authorized			
Officer	902	804	1,706
Enlisted	1,227	1,305	2,532
Total	2,129	2,109	4,238
Assigned			
Officer	604	595	1,199
Enlisted	1,186	1,147	2,333
Total	1,790	1,742	3,532
Percentage of authorized assigned			
Officer	67	74	70
Enlisted	97	90	92
Total	84	83	83

The Individual Ready Reserve (IRR) of the USAR is comprised of Ready Reservists who are not members of units. They are assigned to five categories of control groups: annual training, mobilization designation, reinforcement, delayed, and officer active duty obligor. Control group annual training consists of nonunit Ready Reserve personnel who have a remaining training obligation. Most have two or more years of active duty, and are required to participate in annual active duty training (AT) when directed. Control group mobilization designation consists of nonunit officer personnel who are assigned to authorized key augmentation positions of mobilization tables of distribution and allowances. They are considered to be available upon mobilization or national emergency, and are required to participate in twelve days of annual training, exclusive of travel time, to prepare them for their assignments.

Control group reinforcement is composed of Ready Reserve personnel not in units who have completed the required training portion of their statutory obligation, and also includes members of the Women's Army Corps for whom no appropriate vacancy exists in units. These reservists are not subject to mandatory training requirements.

Control group delayed consists of obligated enlisted personnel who do not enter upon active duty concurrently with their enlistment. They are not authorized or required to participate in any form of training unless specifically directed. Also in this category are Ready Reserve enlisted personnel whose initial entry on active duty or on active duty for training is delayed and who are not required by law or regulation to participate in training in an attached status with a USAR unit. Finally, control group officer active duty obligor consists of officers with active duty obligation who do not enter upon active duty concurrently with their appointment.

As the fiscal year closed, the Individual Ready Reservists in the control group categories described above were assigned as shown in the following table.

	Officers	Enlisted	Total
Annual training	15,864	680,492	696,356
Mobilization designation	4,557	0	4,557
Reinforcement	26,665	184,806	211,471
Delayed	0	7	7
Officer active duty obligor	19,323	1	19,324
Total	66,409	865,306	931,715

In a partial or full mobilization, Individual Ready Reservists would be selected for active duty on a priority basis. Priority group I would consist of individuals with twelve months or less of active duty or active duty for training. Those with no active duty or training would be trained when mobilized and before deployment overseas. Priority group II would consist of those with twelve to twenty-four months of active duty or active duty for training. Priority group III would be those whose active duty and training exceeded two years. Priority group IV would consist of individuals who during their active service were assigned to a hostile area.

Individual members of control group delayed and control group mobilization designation are not available for involuntary order to active duty as reinforcements except when specifically authorized under separate instructions by Headquarters, Department of the Army. During fiscal year 1970, 47,500 officers and enlisted men of the Individual Ready Reserve received training, primarily as fillers for ARNG and USAR units during active duty training and in school and mobilization designation assignments.

Materiel and Supply

Since 1966, annual budget computations of equipment requirements have taken into account the full Army Reserve Components requirements. However, the expansion of the active Army to meet Vietnam demands and the subsequent modernization of Vietnamese forces required the diversion of much of the equipment that would otherwise have been issued to the reserves.

The Reserve Components do not require full allowances of equipment to conduct effective training prior to mobilization, and, consequently, separate requirements for training have been developed. At the end of fiscal year 1969 the Reserve Components had on hand a considerable amount of materiel suitable for training purposes—contingency and training assets—which did not meet operational requirements and would not be used by the reserve units if deployed. However, it was planned that equipment of active Army units that would move to prepositioned equipment overseas would become available to the Reserve Components.

The monetary value of equipment deliveries to the reserves substantially increased during the past few years, from $62 million in fiscal year 1966 to $133 million in fiscal year 1967 and $191 million in fiscal year 1968; in fiscal year 1969, however, the total dropped to $150 million. Equipment deliveries during fiscal year 1970 amounted to $300 million. There have been some concurrent withdrawals to meet Southeast Asia requirements, and the disposal of old equipment further reduced actual stocks.

The Department of the Army does not issue all authorized equipment to the Reserve Components prior to mobilization. The burden would overtax the ability of the units to use, store, and maintain the equipment. Accordingly, the equipment posture of the Reserve Components must be examined under two distinct situations, one for premobilization requirements and the other for postmobilization requirements.

Premobilization training requirements are those equal to or less than full TOE which are considered sufficient to support unit training at home stations during weekend training and at annual training sites. Postmobilization requirements include the remainder of the equipment needed to bring Reserve Component units to full TOE strength and to sustain the Army's approved Reserve Component force when mobilized according to current war and contingency plans.

In the event of a mobilization, the Reserve Components would draw upon three primary sources to bring their equipment to full strength. Located in the United States and in certain oversea areas are equipment stockpiles which would serve partially to supply the ultimate requirements of the Reserve Components. Should active Army forces deploy to their prepositioned equipment sites, the materiel they leave behind would also be available to the activated reserve units. Finally, the reserves would draw directly from factory production for the equipment authorized to them as newly mobilized units.

The high demand for Army aircraft in Southeast Asia will continue to diminish as American forces withdraw and the Vietnamese requirement is satisfied. During the peak war years it had been Department of Defense policy to hold aircraft procurement to levels that would compensate for attrition and anticipate postwar force requirements. While this avoided building excess stocks, it delayed distribution of aircraft to the Reserve Components. As the active Army continues to phase down in Vietnam, the reserve air fleet will undergo a complete modernization.

A portion of the total Reserve Component materiel requirement is for equipment which has only recently been standardized and introduced into the Army supply system. Limited availability of these modernization items permitted issue primarily to the active Army and, with the exception of familiarization training quantities, they were not issued to the Reserve Components during the fiscal year. A pilot program was developed to improve the visibility of requirements for familiarization training in selected, high priority Reserve Component units. This program exercises a management-by-exception technique to override selectively the distribution priority system and meet the familiarization training requirements for the preferred items. Examples of this equipment are combat engineer vehicles, night vision devices, and communications equipment.

During the year the Reserve Components received about $185 million in selected equipment, including helicopters, radar sets, rifles, tanks, and wheeled vehicles, along with enough new communications equipment for familiarization training. Approximately 25 percent of the $185 million was for new items from production.

Consistent with Defense Department instructions to separate active Army and Reserve Component repair and maintenance programs, the Reserve Component backlog in this area was analyzed and budget planning was undertaken with a view to eliminating the arrears by fiscal year 1976. Plans visualize fund allocations that would permit the issue to the Reserve Components in fiscal year 1972 of some $200 million in equipment from depot and maintenance overhaul programs, followed by another $800 million worth during the 1973–76 fiscal year period.

Progress was made during the year in the Mutual Support Training Program, designed to improve training and equipment readiness; to integrate the capability of active and reserve elements; to promote support between active and reserve elements; to facilitate implementation of common systems and organizations; and to familiarize Reserve Component units with new equipment, methods of supply, and techniques. A list of Reserve Component service support units which can be integrated into such a program has been developed and provided to the Army Materiel Command (AMC) for appropriate inclusion in the AMC depot program. The Reserve Component reservoir of trained personnel and the transfer to it of some of the tasks routinely performed by the active Army would help the active Army accomplish its mission. Such arrangements would also increase the readiness of the units of the Reserve Components.

During the fiscal year, a logistic readiness study resulted in the allocation of essential equipment that markedly enhanced the training effectiveness of certain reserve units. These units (primarily combat brigades) received about ninety items of new equipment in sufficient quantity for familiarization training.

Installations and Facilities

Existing Reserve Component facilities, which range from permanently constructed armories and training centers to leased structures of varying adequacy, are used to the maximum extent possible. The current Reserve Component real property inventory is valued at $881.8 million, of which $632.4 million is in Army National Guard facilities and $249.4 million in the Army Reserve. The long-range military construction plan of the Reserve Components provides for replacement of inadequate facilities, expansion of existing facilities to meet space requirements, and replacement by government-owned facilities of leased or donated buildings that are hard to maintain or inadequate for training purposes.

Inventory and stationing plans based on the reorganized structure were reviewed and updated and facility requirements determined. New construction, as well as expansion, alteration, or rehabilitation of existing facilities, was required to provide the plant that is needed for effective operation and training in the Reserve Components.

Military construction funding available during fiscal year 1970 was $36.2 million, of which $16.7 million was obligated. The President's Construction Reduction Plan did not affect the construction for the National Guard since it is a federal grant-aid program. Army Reserve construction was reduced from a programed expenditure of $11.3 million to approximately $4 million, which drastically affected construction planned for the fiscal year. The remaining projects were scheduled for early fiscal year 1971. Based on current costs, unfilled construction requirements for the Reserve Components are estimated at $627 million, which includes construction, expansion, conversion, or rehabilitation of 1,553 armories or centers. Funds available to the Reserve Components for military construction in fiscal year 1970 were as follows:

	ARNG	USAR
	(in millions of dollars)	
New obligation authority	15.0	10.0
Prior-year funds available	6.3	4.9
Funds available	21.3	14.9
Funds obligated	15.0	1.7
Carryover for fiscal year 1971	6.3	13.2

The fiscal year 1970 program called for construction of thirty-eight National Guard armories at a cost of $9.64 million. The Army Reserve program provided for twelve new center facilities and one center expansion at a cost of $9.3 million. The status of armory facilities at year's end was as follows:

	Required	Occupied	Adequate	Requirements [a]
ARNG	2774	2774	1953	821
USAR	1019	1019	287	732

[a] 1,553 existing armories and centers require expansion, conversion, or rehabilitation to meet revised space requirements.

In connection with administrative and logistical support facilities, twenty-four nonarmory projects were finished for the National Guard at an estimated cost of $2.84 million. The Army Reserve does not fund separately for this type facility, since it is constructed as part of a reserve center. Of the 2,200 nonarmory (administrative and logistical) facilities that support the National Guard, 1,906 are considered adequate. The remaining 294 require replacement, expansion, or alteration to correct current deficiencies at a cost of $42.9 million.

Because of the large backlog of inadequate armories and centers required for home station training, the 1970 budget emphasized construction of this type facility. Programed construction for field training facilities at four state-owned or -controlled camps amounted to $1 million in the National Guard program. Insufficient training areas in proper locations for annual training and for local needs.to support training continued to be a problem which has an adverse effect on unit readiness. An inventory of all training areas in the continental United States was analyzed and evaluated at all levels of command. The Department of the Army and the Continental Army Command were acting to delete the least desirable areas and to acquire additional field training areas.

Training

The Reserve Components made progress in training during fiscal year 1970 despite equipment shortages and inadequate training facilities in some areas. Training problems deriving from the 1968 reorganization were overcome in 1970, and retraining of enlisted personnel in new occupational specialties was largely completed; only some hard skill positions whose occupants require over twenty weeks of training remained unfilled.

Participation in unit training continued at a high level during fiscal year 1970. Attendance at unit training assemblies was as follows:

Fiscal Year	Percent ARNG	Percent USAR
1968	97.3	91.8
1969	96.9	91.5
1970	96.6	91.9

The training objective for fiscal years 1969–70 was basic unit training, which includes training through company level. Generally, this objective was met. Several units completed battalion level training. A ten-point Reserve Component improvement program and a program to improve Reserve Component readiness have resulted in improvements in training and will result in more as these programs continue. The round-out concept, a part of the latter program wherein Reserve Component units conduct training as components of major active organizations and receive assistance from them, proved to be of great value to the affected units.

Many personnel of the Reserve Components participated in the Army's educational programs. The following list shows the significance of this individual training effort.

School or Course	Participation ARNG	USAR
Army War College Non-Resident Correspondence Course	22	131
Branch Officer Basic and Advanced and Command and General Staff Correspondence Courses	8,181	7,062
USAR schools	17,710	34,948
Army service and Army area schools	10,481	14,552
State officer candidate schools	2,265	118
Civil Disturbance Orientation Course	97	11
Technician New Equipment Training Course	115	0
Industrial College of the Armed Forces, National Security Management Course (two years)	USAR at USAR school—3,645 USAR in RTU—301	

In fiscal year 1970, the Army National Guard air defense force consisted of twelve battalion headquarters and thirty-eight fire units located in fourteen states. These units represented over 50 percent of the Nike-Hercules groups within the U.S. Army Air Defense Command. Manned by approximately 3,800 National Guard technicians, they were located around selected population and industrial centers and were operational around the clock.

This fiscal year, these Guard units enjoyed the best operational performance record since entering the air defense program in 1954. Two of the units in Los Angeles had perfect scores at the short notice annual practice (SNAP), a feat unprecedented in air defense.

Management

As reduction of the active structure began, increasing reliance was placed on the Reserve Components to fill contingency requirements. Accordingly, a great deal of top management and staff attention was devoted to the problem of the reserves.

A management plan was initiated in the fall of 1969, referred to as the Ten Point Improvement Program for the Reserve Components. Some of the points are directed to the units, some to individuals, and some to the Army Staff. The program is dynamic and is used as a management tool to focus attention on current activities contributing to the readiness of National Guard and U.S. Army Reserve units. A brief description of the ten points follows.

1. Equipment. Included are efforts to increase the flow of equipment to Reserve and National Guard units for essential training. Monthly meetings are held by the Deputy Chief of Staff for Logistics and the Chief, Office of Reserve Components, to resolve problems related to equipment distribution and maintenance support.

2. Home Station Facilities and Training Areas. Included is assessment of requirements for more secure storage areas for the additional equipment, adequacy of nearby training areas—particularly for combat units—and provision of adequate home station facilities, either by expansion of present armories and centers or construction of new buildings.

3. Personnel Recruitment and Retention. Emphasis is on reenlistment of the well-trained, competent citizen-soldier, particularly the young leaders.

4. Personnel Qualifications. Additional professional and technical training requirements are determined and means are sought to permit Army Guardsmen and U.S. Army Reservists to receive personal and unit training.

5. Technicians and Advisers. The key role in unit readiness played by the full-time technician, normally also a member of the

unit, and the adviser, an active Army officer or enlisted man, is recognized.

6. Aviation. Included is a program to increase the number of Reserve Component aviators who have had Vietnam experience as well as to increase the number of modern aircraft available to Guard and Reserve units.

7. Improved Readiness. Various tests and experiments are conducted to explore additional means of increasing the readiness of Guard and Reserve units.

8. One Army Concept. The Army Staff in particular is to include consideration of Reserve Component requirements in Army plans. Also included are plans to insure more active Army participation with Reserve Component units in the field.

9. Public Affairs Program. The objective is to improve the image of the Reserve Components in the eyes of the local communities as well as on a national scale.

10. Management. An effort is made primarily to consolidate the activities listed above, insure balance in the efforts being made, and seek funds to support the program.

The ten-point program was initiated in September 1969 and progress in each of the ten areas is assessed on a monthly basis and reported to the Chief of Staff. Copies of the report go to the U.S. Continental Army Command and Department of the Army staff agencies.

Military Support to Civil Authorities

The ability of the Reserve Components to conduct operations to control civil disturbances was increased during fiscal year 1970; 375,000 National Guardsmen and 14,000 Army Reservists had been trained in riot control as the year closed.

The Army National Guard conducted, at the expense of regular training, sixteen hours of refresher civil disturbance training. Some states also carried out civil disturbance command post exercises in conjunction with local and state civil authorities.

The Army Reserve now has three infantry brigades which are part of the federal military contingency force for the control of civil disturbances. These units also conducted sixteen hours of refresher civil disturbance training at the expense of primary training.

This additional responsibility of the Reserve Components calls for their immediate availability in times of natural disasters, civil disturbances, and other emergencies. The Army National Guard bears the brunt of these requirements because of its responsibility to the respective state governments. From July 1, 1969, to June 30,

1970, individual National Guard units were called in by state governors on ninety-two different occasions in thirty-one states and the District of Columbia. These included civil disturbances at Chicago, Illinois; Madison, Wisconsin; Charleston, South Carolina; Berkeley, California; and Columbus and Kent, Ohio. Guardsmen were also called in during natural disasters, including a forest fire in Carson City, Nevada, a hurricane in St. Petersburg, Florida, a tornado in Mobile, Alabama, a blizzard in Nebraska, and floods in California, Iowa, and North and South Dakota. A sampling of the variety of general emergencies that required National Guard assistance includes explosions and fires in Noel, Missouri, a search for a missing person in Tofte, Minnesota, train derailments in Piedmont, West Virginia, and Glendora, Mississippi, the war moratorium in Washington, D.C., snow emergencies in Vermont and New York, and avalanche control in Stevens Pass, Washington.

When a crisis exists affecting the welfare of the nation, the federal government assumes control and may call on the Army Reserves as well as National Guard forces, as in the case of the postal strike in New York City. On that occasion, the Army Reserve furnished eighty-seven units with an assigned strength of 10,300 troops and the National Guard ten units with an assigned strength of 10,912 troops, of which 5,175 Army Reservists and 6,839 National Guardsmen were assigned to postal activities on the peak day of operation. This action was fortunately short-lived; the strikers returned to their duties in a matter of days.

VII. Management, Budget, and Funds

Organizational Developments

There were several organizational developments in diverse areas during fiscal year 1970. To capitalize on rapid advances being made in sensor, automatic data processing, and communications technology, an Army surveillance, target acquisition, and night observation (STANO) management structure was established on July 15, 1969. It consists of four elements: a STANO steering group headed by the Army's Vice Chief of Staff and including heads of departmental staff agencies and deputy commanders of major continental U.S. commands to provide broad guidance; a STANO systems manager and office within the office of the Army Chief of Staff to direct, co-ordinate, and expedite staff and major command actions in the STANO field; STANO offices within the departmental staff and major continental U.S. commands to centralize STANO activities within these organizations; and an operationally oriented test and evaluation facility at Fort Hood, Texas—Mobile Army Sensor Systems Test, Evaluation and Review (Project MASSTER) —established on October 1, 1969, with testing getting under way in February 1970. Under Project MASSTER, field tests of materiel and related systems are to be conducted to evaluate the potential of hardware and determine its impact on organization, concepts, and doctrine in the land combat system.

A STANO division was also established in the Office of the Chief of Research and Development to supervise research and development in connection with night vision, radar, sensors, and special purpose detectors (see chapter 9).

In another organizational development, the Assistant Chief of Staff for Intelligence requested and was granted relief of certain operational responsibilities connected with supervision of a number of class II activities. To permit the Army's top intelligence office to concentrate on staff functions, seven class II activities were transferred to the U.S. Army Intelligence Command during the period September 12–December 31, 1969. Another five were consolidated into one activity called the Intelligence Control Group on January 15, 1970, and on April 15, 1970, the U.S. Army Liaison Office of the Tactical Air Reconnaissance Center was discontinued, leaving only three class II activities under the Office of the Assistant Chief of Staff for Intelligence.

Two independent Army studies made in 1968 and 1969 pointed out the need for the Comptroller of the Army to improve his organization in the Washington area in order to reflect the growing impact of automatic data processing and management information technology on financial management and reporting systems. In addition, manpower strength reductions were directed in fiscal year 1970. As a result of these influences, the U.S. Army Finance and Comptroller Information Systems Command was established on May 24, 1970. This command is a class II activity under the Comptroller of the Army and represents a consolidation of selected departmental elements within the Office, Comptroller of the Army, and two of his class II activities. The command provides central direction to finance and accounting functions Army-wide, prescribes applicable policies and procedures for financial management systems, operates a central bank for financial management data, provides automatic data processing (ADP) support to selected staff agencies, and provides finance services to Department of the Army military and civilian personnel.

Management Programs and Systems

In essence, resource related planning has as its mission the task of insuring that all possible program alternatives are explored and that the Army's resource management system provides necessary guidance. In the past year, potential budget levels were examined, and alternative investment and manpower programs that could be funded were developed and reviewed by the Army Staff. By the close of the fiscal year it appeared that the hoped-for phaseover from a Southeast Asia–oriented Army budget to a peacetime budget permitting a reasonable rate of modernization of the Army's equipment had been aided by resource related planning.

During 1968 it had become clear that defense expenditures in general, and Army funding in particular, would begin to feel the pinch as the United States phased down its Southeast Asia role and as domestic needs were accorded higher and higher priority. To evolve a sound analytic approach to the problem of developing a total Army budget during the expected period of constrained funding, the Secretary of the Army in January 1969 chartered a special study group in the Office of the Chief of Staff to examine the impact of reduced postwar budget levels. This effort, which came to be known as resource related planning, began to have application in late 1969, and in early 1970 it served to provide over-all guidance in the development of the Army's program for the fiscal year 1972–76 period.

In addition to earlier and improved analysis of funding choices, substantial procedural revisions were made in the Army's resource management system. These revisions had first application in the analysis of the fiscal year 1971 budget and the fiscal year 1972–76 Army program, but it is anticipated that lessons learned will be profitably applied in the continuing effort to develop Army programs that make the best use of available funds.

An ad hoc Army financial management committee was convened during the period January 15–27, 1970, to examine and recommend improvements in Army organization and procedures for financial management. The Comptroller of the Army chaired the committee, which included representatives of the offices of the Assistant Vice Chief of Staff, the Deputy Chief of Staff for Personnel, the Deputy Chief of Staff for Logistics, and the Assistant Chief of Staff for Force Development.

In its analyses, the committee placed particular emphasis on the Army's ability to respond rapidly and effectively under the revised planning, programing, and budgeting system (PPBS) that became effective January 1, 1970. The revised system curtails the use of the program change request (PCR) as the primary vehicle for submission of recommended program changes, and provides that each military department will submit a program objective memorandum (POM), which will express program requirements within fiscal and logistic guidance issued by the Secretary of Defense.

Changes in Army financial management, stemming from the committee's recommendations, will accomplish the following improvements:

1. Formalize and document the direction of the programing function; retain it in the Office of the Assistant Vice Chief of Staff; redesignate the Director, Force Planning Analysis, as Director, Planning and Programing Analysis; and improve the analytical staff of that office to facilitate continuing critical analysis of the total Army program.

2. Replace the Program Budget Advisory Committee with the Select Committee, which has membership at the Deputy Chief of Staff level and is supported by two new subordinate committees—the Program Guidance and Review Committee and the Budget Review Committee—to enhance and expedite decision-making in the area of resource management.

3. Broaden the authority of the Director of the Army Budget to address all Army appropriations; establish a new resource review

and analysis group to provide the ability to effectively challenge budget submissions; and, concurrently, transfer responsibility for direction of the operation and maintenance, Army (OMA), appropriation from the Director of Army Budget to his Assistant Director for Operations.

The Keystone Management Systems Steering Committee, composed of general officers and chaired by the Assistant Vice Chief of Staff, continued efforts to improve the Army's basic resource management systems. The committee centered its attention on systems that affect authorizations and related personnel and equipment asset reporting.

The Weapon System Acquisition Improvement Program was directed toward preventing cost growth in the life cycle of weapon system acquisition by improving estimate procedures, controlling changes, assessing technical risk, exercising competitive procedures, and improving test and evaluation procedures. Immediate improvement was sought in all of these areas, while long-range attention was directed to the validation of cost estimates, project management, system definition, source selection, contractor performance measurement, and contract changes.

Selected acquisition reports—comprehensive, quarterly status reports of major systems managed within the Department of Defense—are the key recurring summaries received by the Secretary of the Army on the progress of designated systems and are the vehicles by which this progress is reported to the Office of the Secretary of Defense and to the Congress. They are prepared by project offices within the Army Materiel Command and are reviewed by the Department of the Army Staff and the Office of the Assistant Vice Chief. When the final report is forwarded to the Office of the Secretary of Defense, copies are returned to the originator, thus completing the management loop.

Selected acquisition reports summarize current estimates of operational and technical performance levels, milestone completion dates, and program costs. These current estimates are compared with the original plan and current program and any variance, such as schedule slippage or cost growth, is identified and explained. The selected acquisition report, although not a decision document, is a management tool designed to uncover problems and focus attention on matters which require decision by top management. It provides rapid insight and fosters greater understanding of complex systems which take years to develop. A selected acquisition report highlights program changes, funding requirements, and cost overruns, among other things.

In the past, estimates have varied from week to week and from agency to agency. The selected acquisition report now forces servicewide agreement on a unique set of estimates at a particular point in time. It provides a common reference point which makes it easier to reconcile one document with another.

Because of the increasing use of automated data processing in management activities, the Army in October 1969 published a master plan for the design and development of Army management information systems. This plan sets forth in some detail the framework within which all Army ADP (automatic data processing) management systems will be developed in the 1970–80 decade, assigning developmental priorities and employing a pyramidal model to emphasize the multidimensional problems associated with this development.

During the past year, the Army continued to develop a cohesive logistic management information system. Within this system are four guidance and reporting subsystems including the Supply, Maintenance, and Readiness Management Information System; the Integrated Transportation Management Information System; the Integrated Support Services Management Information System; and the Integrated Facilities Management Information System.

In the area of supply and maintenance, efforts were concentrated on expanding the design project to establish an integrated supply, maintenance, and materiel readiness reporting system into an approved plan for Army-wide implementation. Under this plan, the flow of management information from unit level up through intervening echelons to Headquarters, Department of the Army, would be dependent upon the collection, processing, and storage of management data and the output to management at all echelons. The implementation plan was published and co-ordinated within the Army Staff. The comments received as a result of this co-ordination were being evaluated as the year closed.

Further progress was also achieved in the development of the three other subsystems of the over-all Logistics Management Information System. Through a project designed to provide increased Army management at selected transportation echelons, the Stanford Research Institute provided support by conducting a study to determine the essential elements of information and management indicators required for the effective management of Army transportation. In the mission area of the Chief of Support Services, work continued on the development of functional system requirements for the property disposal portion of the Support Services Management Information System. The purpose of this system is to provide information to measure performance, budgeting, and management of various logistic services, including food service, commissary operations, clothing sales, clothing issues, laundry and dry cleaning operations, and property disposal. As the year ended the functional system requirements for the property disposal portion of the overall system were being staffed within Headquarters, Department of the Army, and with the major Army commands.

Development continued during the year on an integrated facilities system capable of providing accurate and timely information on Army real property resources and programs. Such information is needed by the Army Staff to develop costs associated with various courses of action, to reach decisions related to force structure, force readiness, and facilities planning and programing, and to provide functional managers and commanders at all echelons with the information required to manage real property.

In March 1970 the Warehousing Gross Performance Measurement System (WGPMS) and the Defense Integrated Management Engineering Systems (DIMES) were integrated. With this integration, manpower performance and utilization became an integral part of the total work planning and control, accounting, manpower, and budget systems. The integration places increased emphasis on method improvements and improved productivity. Army implementation delineates policies and responsibilities and applies to activities engaged in providing products and services such as supply depots, maintenance depots, inventory control points, terminals, shipyards and arsenals, industrially funded activities which utilize standard cost methods and engineered performance standards, and other selected activities determined by each Department of Defense (DOD) component. Subsequent to this action, DOD components indicated that the benefits and savings from the DIMES effort had not received proper recognition. As a result, in addition to examples of tangible savings which were rejected by the auditors for the cost reduction program, the Office of the Secretary of Defense was provided with examples which were not submitted because local interpretation considered they would not meet the criteria. Also, criteria were furnished that could be uniformly applied and result in more DIMES savings and benefits applicable to the cost reduction program.

In the last quarter of fiscal year 1969 the Department of Defense initiated a comprehensive servicewide system, called the Logistics Performance Measurement and Evaluation System, to improve the management of Defense installations and logistics. The system is a procedure for evaluating performance, identifying problems, initiating corrective actions, and setting goals. During fiscal year 1970, the first complete program year, the Army evaluated performance in twenty functional areas worldwide relating to materiel, procurement, maintenance, transportation, and facilities management. Where deficiencies were identified, actions were taken to redistribute the work load and adjust resources so that they were applied to the more essential activities.

Although the primary missions of installations vary, certain functions are common to them all. Installation commanders in every case are responsible for industrial-type operations involving real property, supply, maintenance, and other logistic services, and for city-manager-type activities such as dependent schools, service clubs, open messes, and recreational facilities. To promote efficiency and economy in installation operation, the Army in fiscal year 1970 developed basic doctrine, philosophy, procedures, and controls for installation management and standard organization for each type of class I installation. With post support and community activities standardized, the Army will have a common basis for training and assigning personnel to garrison duties, uniform command management standards for installation comparison, and a foundation for professional competition between installations.

The closeout of a number of installations under the general retrenchment related to American withdrawal from Vietnam left some installation commanders without adequate local resources to fulfill logistic support commitments. The impact upon the Interservice Logistic Support Program was substantial and led to a comprehensive study of the policies and principles of interservice, interdepartmental, and interagency support, which will be completed in the coming fiscal year.

The Army Commercial and Industrial Activities Program was also affected by the general curtailment. The necessity to conserve funds and manpower led major commands to re-evaluate installation support programs and select means that were less costly to the government. These actions generated increased interest in commercial and industrial activities and resulted in numerous inquiries from congressional committees, employee unions, and trade associations for justification of actions taken to convert activities to other methods of operation.

A deficiency identification system was implemented in the past year to make audit results useful on more than an individual report basis. The system includes the publication of automated print-outs, which highlight functional areas with the greatest concentration of deficiencies disclosed in audit reports, their monetary impact, and those that are repeats. The presentation of data in this format enables staff agencies and commands to identify problem areas at a glance and schedule corrective actions in order of priority and where the greater economies may be achieved.

An evaluation of the Army Study System was completed during the fiscal year and recommendations were implemented on January 1, 1970. New procedures were developed that will make the system more responsive to the needs of Army managers, identify subjects that should receive early study attention, insure that adequate resources are assigned to priority studies, and improve the over-all management of the study system.

Budget and Funds

The Army's budget request for regular appropriations for fiscal year 1970 totaled $30,050.9 million in new obligational authority. Following reviews by the Office of the Secretary of Defense and the Bureau of the Budget, the President requested $25,929.5 million for the Army, and the Congress appropriated $22,446.2 million. The chronological development of this budget is traced in the table on the following page. A later supplemental budget produced an additional $1,134.9 million.

DEPARTMENT OF THE ARMY
BUDGET OUTLAYS FISCAL YEARS 1968, 1969, 1970

(In thousands of dollars)

	Fiscal Year 1968	Fiscal Year 1969	Fiscal Year 1970
Military personnel, Army	7,765,096	8,460,678	8,590,000
Reserve personnel, Army	254,312	270,796	310,000
National Guard personnel, Army	312,714	315,913	370,000
Operation and maintenance, Army	7,929,545	8,029.939	7,460,000
Operation and maintenance, ARNG	243,731	269,734	307,000
National Board for the Promotion of Rifle Practice	350	38	50
Procurement of equipment and missiles, Army	5,841,011	6,116,741	5,339,900
Research, development, test, and evaluation, Army	1,434,096	1,520,840	1,640,000
Military Construction, Army	674,047	450,324	451,100
Military Construction, ARNG	3,709	8,377	7,700
Military Construction, AR	231	1,508	9,000
Army Stock Fund	180,553	—305,119	—107,000
Army Industrial Fund	609,633	—34,958	—9,600
Army Management Fund	13,954	—7,802	....
Consolidated Working Fund	129	—1	....
Miscellaneous expired accounts	31,154	....	....
Subtotal	25,294,265	25,097,008	24,467,150
Army trust funds	406	82	86
Trust revolving funds	—4,770	2,042	2,174
Miscellaneous receipts	—67,128	—63,864	—67,611
Total budget outlays	25,222,773	25,035,268	24,401,799

The central fiscal agencies of the federal government continued to emphasize the need for priority attention to accrual accounting and reporting. The General Accounting Office and the Office of the Secretary of Defense conducted separate surveys within the military

DEPARTMENT OF THE ARMY
CHRONOLOGY OF THE FISCAL YEAR 1970 BUDGET

New Obligational Authority [a]

(In millions of dollars)

Program Element	DA Submission to OSD	President's Budget	Enacted	Supplemental Budget
			(PL 91-171)	
Military personnel, Army	8,754.3	8,535.0	8,107.0	768.4
Reserve personnel, Army	338.0	311.0	306.7	32.0
National Guard personnel, Army	364.0	363.5	356.8	46.6
Operation and maintenance, Army	8,713.3	7,596.0	7,214.4	253.3
Operation and maintenance, Army National Guard	326.0	306.0	297.8	17.2
National Board for the Promotion of Rifle Practice	......	......	.5	......
Procurement of equipment and missiles, Army	8,177.8	5,933.0	4,254.4	4.9
Research, development, test, and evaluation, Army	1,981.2	1,822.5	1,596.8	11.5
Subtotal excluding construction	(28,654.6)	(24,867.0)	(22,134.0)	(1,133.9)
			(PL 91-142)	
Military Construction, Army	1,356.3	1,037.5	287.2	1.0
Military Construction, Army Reserve	20.0	10.0	10.0	......
Military Construction, Army National Guard	20.0	15.0	15.0	......
Subtotal, construction accounts	(1,396.3)	(1,062.5)	(312.2)	(1.0)
Total new obligational authority	30,050.9	25,929.5	22,446.2	1,134.9

[a] Figures may not add due to rounding.

departments to determine the propriety and effectiveness of implementation procedures and to identify and resolve problem areas. These and other related actions should result in achieving the ability to present and support the budget for fiscal year 1972 on the basis of accrued revenues and expenditures.

The Army placed increased emphasis on cost analysis in evaluating alternatives among weapons systems and forces. A systematic examination of the costs of interrelated activities and equipment makes it possible to determine the relative costs of alternative systems, organizations, and force structures. The Army applied cost analysis techniques to such areas as weapon and support systems, communications systems, force structures, and force units, as well as to materiel systems, theater Army, and total Army costs. Such analyses have been conducted in connection with a Safeguard system review; with the publication of handbooks related to redeployment and force change costs; with the surface-to-air (SAM-D) projects; with planning operations such as the Joint Strategic Objective Plan; and with estimating methodology. To improve the technique, training courses were developed or improved at Defense and Army levels during the year.

Economic analysis also received increased attention. In 1969 the Department of Defense issued instructions covering economic analysis of proposed Department of Defense investments, which substantially broadened the range of problems on which a formal economic analysis is required. The Army issued its implementing regulation in June 1969, and in late 1969 extended the requirements for economic analysis into the fields of weapons systems and research projects for the first time. Economic analysis played an important role in the evaluation of base closures, such as the case of the Army Pictorial Center. It will make a substantial contribution to the Long-Range Stationing Study, under way at the end of the fiscal year, and was applied to major construction, fuel conversion, and such management systems as the integrated facilities system.

Based on data collected in Vietnam, the U.S. Army Field Operating Cost Agency provided the Army with detailed information on the operating costs of the 25th Infantry Division and the 1st Cavalry Division (Airmobile), including their normal slice of combat support and combat service support for fiscal year 1969. Selected Vietnamese units and U.S. units in Korea, Germany, and the continental United States were similarly analyzed.

Despite fiscal constraints, career attractiveness and the soldier's standard of living remained matters of major concern and attention. Some twenty personnel support programs were reviewed to determine the impact of financial restrictions, and it was found that services had been reduced or temporarily suspended in a few instances. Indications were that deterioration would continue unless corrective measures were taken immediately. Three activities were chosen for immediate attention: medical service, commissary store operations, and laundry and dry cleaning services. These activities provide significant financial advantage to the individual and affect a large portion of the dependent and retired population. About $35 million in additional support was directed to these three major areas, and the Army Staff was directed to plan longer range improvements involving management, construction, and renovation of facilities. Support of these programs was to be governed by certain principles: services at acceptable standards must be supplied to all eligible personnel; appropriate funds and personnel spaces must be earmarked for these programs and the integrity of the earmarked resources preserved; resources support of these activities must be removed from competition with support for mission-type activities; and living standard requirements must be considered as the fixed cost of supporting a soldier, on a par with pay and not subject to reduction below acceptable levels.

Curtailment of resources had an effect on statistical information in the Army, and a number of services had to be reduced or eliminated. The Army Pocket Data Book was eliminated, and statistical surveys, sampling methods and techniques, and special statistical studies and consultative and advisory services had to be reduced.

As a part of the program of the Secretary of the Army to improve weapon system acquisition, the Army initiated Project ICE (improved cost estimates). This project has the dual purpose of providing valid cost estimates on specific systems and developing methodology and expertise for use in formulating estimates on other systems.

In the first phase of Project ICE the Army established five special task groups at separate commodity commands of the Army Materiel Command to perform life cycle cost estimates on selected systems. The first five systems were Lance, the M–60A1E2 tank, the armored reconnaissance scout vehicle, the Army area communications system, and the utility tactical transport aircraft system. The end products of these task groups were being reviewed and validated as the year closed, to assure a life cycle cost estimate with pertinent information for management decisions.

The second phase of Project ICE included seven additional systems and more deeply involves the project manager in preparing the estimate. Systems included in this phase are the heavy lift helicopter, the improved Hawk, the mechanized infantry combat vehicle, the Bushmaster, and TACFIRE.

The recently begun third phase of Project ICE includes eight systems and is being carried out by the project managers. By performing the estimate, the project manager will be better able to relate the estimate to future managerial decisions. Systems included in phase three are the Cobra, the mobile assault bridge, 152-mm. ammunition, the TOW antitank missile, the Gama Goat, the Dragon antitank missile, the XM198 howitzer, and selected night vision equipment.

The Army phase of the Joint Uniform Military Pay System (JUMPS-Army) progressed satisfactorily toward its implementation date of January 1, 1972. JUMPS is applicable to all components of the Department of Defense. However, each service will develop its own system and use data processing equipment peculiar to the unique characteristics of that system.

All pay accounts for military personnel on active duty with the Army will be maintained on magnetic tape at the Finance Center, U.S. Army (FCUSA), Fort Benjamin Harrison, Indiana, from the time an individual enters the Army to the time he is separated from the Army. Changes in pay will be forwarded to FCUSA via electrical communications from the member's station. Automatic data processing equipment will be used to post pay changes to individual accounts, to produce payrolls, to issue checks, and to prepare statements of leave and earnings.

Active pay accounts have been tested using the JUMPS procedures during the past five years. Actual payments, in check or cash at the option of the individual, have been made based on computations by the JUMPS computer. Definitive savings cannot be identified until all pay accounts are under JUMPS-Army. The peculiarities of processing incidental to the extraordinary movement of accounts into and out of the test environment preclude a factual determination of savings until such unique conditions are removed.

To an increasing extent the Army relies on independent, management-type, internal audit as a reliable means of appraising the effectiveness of its use of resources. In fiscal year 1970, with guidance provided by the Army Staff Audit Priorities Committee, the U.S. Army Audit Agency (USAAA) emphasized the programing and performance of audit work oriented toward specific problems.

In Vietnam, the requests of Army commanders were a primary consideration in audit scheduling. To take maximum advantage of limited audit resources, a policy of restricting audits to ninety days elapsed time was followed. It is expected that audit activity will continue at a high level. Cessation or reduction of hostilities and the withdrawal of U.S. troops will initially increase rather than decrease audit requirements.

As a part of the problem-oriented approach, the Army Audit Agency increased its use of flash reports whereby commanders directly concerned were notified immediately of audit findings and recommendations where prompt corrective action was advisable. These flash reports frequently resulted in significant savings in dollars and improvements in operations.

In the area of cost reduction, the Army Audit Agency continued to validate savings claimed in operations by Army activities in order to assure that savings were accurate in accordance with Department of Defense standards.

During the year, the rate of change from manual to automated management systems, both on department and command levels, continued to accelerate. Many of these systems provide the primary source of information on which the management of Army resources—men, money, and materials—is based. Due to dependence upon the computer and the trend toward standardized computer systems, audit methods are undergoing major change. The Army Audit Agency recognized that an automated management system has to be reviewed during its design stage to assure that management needs are met and an efficient and responsive audit approach is developed. Accordingly, a systems audit division was established in Headquarters, USAAA, for the purpose of implementing audit participation in the development of major Army management and automatic data processing systems.

Also during the year, the Army Audit Agency performed a study of alternative means of auditing officer and noncommissioned officer open messes on a worldwide basis. In the future, open mess audits, which traditionally have been command responsibilities, will be conducted alternately by public accounting firms and by the Army Audit Agency.

Cost Reduction Program

Progress in the cost reduction program continued during fiscal year 1970, when $441.8 million was saved against a goal of $341 million. The actions taken in fiscal year 1970 were estimated to have a three-year savings of $843.8 million for fiscal years 1970–72 against a goal of $675 million. Several examples illustrate how the program has operated.

The Army saved $135,200 by obtaining a change in government

specifications for containers used to ship ammunition within the United States. After the specification change, the Army was able to utilize stock which had previously been considered excess.

Delay assemblies were being rejected in acceptance tests for excessive burning time and then scrapped. A value engineering study revealed that the units could be disassembled and the primer section replaced. Fiscal year 1970 savings will total $543,000.

Finally, the nose body assembly for the M126 bomb was previously cast from magnesium by a permanent mold method. An engineering study disclosed that savings amounting to $696,300 could be achieved in fiscal year 1970 by producing the nose assembly from extruded magnesium.

Because of the current period of austerity, greater emphasis has been placed on the need to obtain maximum efficiency from available resources.

Watervliet Arsenal, New York, was selected by the Office of the Secretary of Defense (OSD) to receive an outstanding unit award, and the Vice President of the United States made the presentation during the OSD cost reduction and management improvement program awards ceremony held on October 28, 1969. Selection was based on the outstanding support given the cost reduction program by the arsenal's top management, good program administrative practices, a low audit invalidation rate (2 percent), and significant savings in relation to size, mission, and operating budget.

In addition to the outstanding unit award, individual awards were presented by the Vice President to Lieutenant Colonel James R. Vance of Fort Rucker, Alabama; Lionel P. Hernholm of the U.S. Army Combat Developments Command, Fort Belvoir, Virginia; and David E. Ciruli of the Pueblo Army Depot, Pueblo, Colorado. Seven individuals were nominated but not selected by OSD for awards, one individual was selected for special consideration, and two Army organizations were honored at a Chief of Staff awards ceremony on February 10, 1970, to recognize over-all excellence of unit cost reduction programs as well as noteworthy individual savings accomplishments.

VIII. Logistics

An Army logistics offensive was launched in fiscal year 1970. In a broad sense, the offensive is an Army-wide program to re-emphasize logistic principles, update and refine techniques, revise systems, and more clearly define training and career management objectives. The offensive was geared to support the four broad objectives stressed by the Chief of Staff—mission, motivation, modernization, and management.

General Creighton W. Abrams used the term "logistics offensive" at Phu Bai, Vietnam, in the spring of 1969 to describe what was required throughout the Army logistic system in Vietnam. He meant it as a compliment for the impressive improvement that had been made in all areas of logistics. In reality, he was issuing a challenge to professional logisticians when, as the senior combat commander in the field, he applied the term "offensive" to a military logistic operation.

Even as substantial progress has been made under the offensive to improve the Army's logistic system, many areas have been isolated that require improvement. Actions were taken in fiscal year 1970 to insure that the American soldier gets "what he needs, where and when he needs it, and in the condition required for his use."

In February 1970 an Army logistic policy council was formed, comprised of general officers representing major activities worldwide, to advise and assist the departmental headquarters in evaluating and developing logistic policy, logistic systems standardization, and logistic concepts to improve the Army logistic system.

Materiel Acquisition

For the last decade the procurement objectives for materiel support for the general purpose forces of all the military services have been determined by the Secretary of Defense and stated in his annual logistic guidance. Army budget submissions must support the guidance objectives. The guidance establishes a balance between programed forces and the inventories of equipment, ammunition, secondary items, and consumables to sustain them in combat. For the Army, it specifies the number of division force equivalents to be equipped and supported.

The logistic guidance divides Army forces into categories and establishes logistic objectives tailored for the planned strategic employment of each force category.

In issuing his guidance the Secretary of Defense has consistently directed that all U.S. forces in Vietnam be fully equipped and supplied and be supported by a full pipeline to replace consumption and attrition. These forces are now being fully sustained by deliveries from the active production base, and the 1970 budget request provided for this support through the next budget year.

The table below shows total obligational authority for equipment and ammunition procurement programs by category and year since fiscal year 1965. The growth trend through fiscal year 1969 is reversed in 1970, a reflection of the reduction in estimated consumption rates in Southeast Asia. Fiscal year 1969 funding for direct support of the U.S. Southeast Asia effort was $4.9 billion; the comparable figure for fiscal year 1970 is $3.3 billion, a reduction of 33 percent.

The $6 billion in contracts awarded during fiscal year 1970 included $4.9 billion for the Army ($3.7 billion from current year and $1.2 billion from prior-year funds) and $1.1 billion for customers who buy and use Army equipment and ammunition. Sufficient ammunition was procured in the fiscal year to meet fixed Army requirements, assuming that anticipated Southeast Asia withdrawals take place.

ARMY PROCUREMENT PROGRAM
(In millions of dollars)

Program	Fiscal Years					
	1965	1966	1967	1968	1969	1970
Aircraft	338	1,043	914	959	659	385
Aircraft spares	49	255	239	298	152	77
Missiles	235	305	346	454	850	767
Missile spares	14	45	26	25	45	39
Weapons and combat vehicles	215	539	608	587	509	287
Tactical and support vehicles	345	540	571	399	390	424
Communications and electronics	204	478	590	589	589	345
Other support equipment	151	415	632	383	440	270
Ammunition	334	1,317	1,279	2,239	2,913	1,731
Production base support	77	206	297	337	170	341
Total	1,962	5,143	5,502	6,270	6,717	4,666

As a result of deliveries from procurement, the estimated value of principal items on hand at the end of the fiscal year was $20.9 billion. This decrease in assets from $21.7 billion in 1969 is the result of the high cost of Vietnam operations and Vietnamization and a decrease in total deliveries from $8.4 billion in 1969 to $6.4 billion in 1970.

In a period of competing demands for funds for both military and domestic needs, and with the pressures of inflation and the threat of cost overruns, effective use of public funds is essential. Weapon systems are especially costly, and to insure that the money spent on them is used to full advantage, the Army made a detailed study of the weapon system acquisition process. New control techniques were developed which represent a significant departure from former practices.

One of the first actions was to adopt a "should cost" analysis technique. In the commercial field, price competition stimulates efficient practices. In the area of defense procurement there is less pressure for efficiency, and in the case of sole source procurement, the incentive declines even further. Thus the government, as the purchaser, must insure that proposed costs represent what a contractor should incur assuming reasonable efficiency. Under new procedures developed from the study, analysis of a contractor's proposal against a number of actions in progress will provide a contracting officer with negotiating background.

The study also revealed the need for a management information system that would measure contract performance, weigh actual costs against planned costs, and identify problems as early as possible. It also confirmed the need to improve the methods of developing performance specifications to reduce technical risks, all with a view to minimizing redirections and contract changes, which contribute to cost growth.

The Cheyenne helicopter project is an example in weapon system acquisition of the problems of cost, contract performance, performance specification, and technical risk. In fiscal year 1966 the Army contracted with the Lockheed Aircraft Corporation for the development of an advanced aerial fire support system. The central component of the system is the Cheyenne helicopter (AH–56). Pursuant to an option clause in the development contract, a separate contract was negotiated on January 8, 1967, for the production of 375 aircraft. On May 19, 1969, the production contract was terminated by the Army for default. Lockheed appealed to the Armed Services Board of Contract Appeals, alleging that the Army erred and claiming an estimated $150 million as damages. The appeal, pending as the year closed, should be acted upon in fiscal year 1971. The Army formed a litigation group under the supervision of the General Counsel to present the Army's case.

Meanwhile, the development program continued during fiscal year 1970 and considerable progress was reported in resolving most of the technical problems that caused termination of the production contract. On March 3, 1970, however, Lockheed stated that it had exhausted its operating capital because of the size of its claims against the Department of Defense under this and other contracts and requested the Office of the Secretary of Defense (OSD) to provide relief pending settlement of the claims. As the year closed, the request was receiving careful study by the Office of the Secretary of Defense. The Army was particularly concerned with the effects of possible OSD action on further Cheyenne development and upon its plans eventually to purchase the advanced aerial fire support system. A decision on procurement of Cheyennes was deferred. The deferment will permit additional development and further evaluation of alternatives. The Lockheed financial request and the Cheyenne program received wide publicity.

Looking ahead to procurement of materiel in future years, the physical condition of the industrial facilities that are needed to support Army production has become a matter of primary concern. The Army owns a production base that consists largely of ammunition plants that were designed and constructed, for the most part, during World War II and the Korean War. Some of the manufacturing processes being used date back as far as World War I. This base has been severely taxed by intense operations during three major conflicts. Processes have become grossly inefficient and, indeed, unsafe, and working conditions in some instances are poor.

The Army developed a program in 1968 to rehabilitate and modernize this base; the work is to be carried out over the course of several years at an estimated cost of $2.3 billion. The demands of the Vietnam War have limited initial expenditures to $208 million and $119 million in fiscal years 1970 and 1971 respectively. Funding is essential if the production capability is to be kept responsive to future emergency needs.

Materiel Maintenance

To focus attention on the ever-widening gap between required maintenance skills and the complexity of equipment, and to improve resource management and the operational readiness of materiel, the Army established a project called Maintenance Support Positive (MS+). The current concept of performing maintenance as far forward as possible, coupled with piece and part repair and replacement, has required excessive proliferation of parts, special skills, and sophisticated test equipment at all levels of maintenance and has proven to be extremely costly. The new concept emphasizes component replacement in operating units rather than piece part repair, thereby reducing requirements for highly skilled personnel and sophisticated equipment at all levels of maintenance. The program will also evaluate generally all of the Army's materiel maintenance activities, policies, and practices.

In April 1970, new instructions were issued prescribing standards for Army equipment worldwide. The standards relate to three categories of conditions: operationally ready, not operationally ready because of supply shortages, and not operationally ready because of maintenance work to be done. The standards are measures of equipment and logistic support performance, including delays for parts or maintenance.

In converting from The Army Equipment Records System to The Army Maintenance Management System (TAMMS) in October 1969, the Army preserved the standard record-keeping system, but made major changes in the requirements to process maintenance data by reducing reportable line items from 556 to 297. Among other benefits, TAMMS requires 25,000,000 fewer punch cards and 193 less man-years of key punch effort at the installation level, representing an estimated annual saving of $1.1 million.

Depot materiel maintenance and support activities amounted to $781.5 million in direct expenses in fiscal year 1970. Of the total, $616.8 million was used for depot maintenance activities, $6.6 million for base operations costs, $6 million for technical, administrative, and new equipment maintenance training, and $152.1 million for maintenance support activities.

The Seventh and Eighth Worldwide Depot Maintenance Programing Conferences were held at Rosslyn, Virginia, in December 1969 and June 1970 to revise the 1970 and review the 1971 and 1972 depot maintenance programs in the light of revised requirements, updated plans, and projected funding levels. All programs were adjusted and approved.

Conferences were also held to develop programs for the support of Army forces in Vietnam, Korea, Thailand, Okinawa, and Europe under the closed loop support system, the program established in 1966 to provide intensive management over selected items through the entire cycle of withdrawal, overhaul, and return to the Army supply system. As the year ended the program included ninety-seven major end items and sixty-four secondary items. Approximately 5,000 individual major and secondary items were withdrawn from and returned to Vietnam monthly under program schedules established for that command alone.

Aviation Logistics

Standardization is one of the more effective ways of reducing the range of needed repair parts, ground support equipment, avionics, armament, special tools, and personnel skills. A program to standardize the Army aircraft fleet worldwide was in progress during the year. It is designed to reduce the number of different missions, designs, and series of aircraft by command, consistent with operational requirements. By year's end, reductions had been made in Korea, Japan, Europe, and the Canal Zone.

Operational readiness standards were established at 80 percent for fixed wing and 75 percent for rotary wing aircraft in fiscal year 1970, with a weighted average of 76 percent for all aircraft. The year was one of high-level aviation activity. Army aircraft—a large percentage of them helicopters—flew over 550,000 hours in April 1970, one of the highest flying hour months in Army aviation history. It is interesting to note that, while achieving these flying hours, helicopters averaged 73 percent and fixed wing 79 percent in readiness, for an average of 74 percent.

With a fleet of over 12,000 aircraft, the Army aviation program consumes nearly half of the funds required by the Army for depot maintenance. To achieve a balanced work load in depot maintenance at the least cost, the Army overhauls about 65 percent of its first-line aircraft in Department of Defense activities, including the Naval Air Station at Pensacola, Florida. The remainder are overhauled by prime manufacturers.

The large number of aircraft in Vietnam has challenged Army management and led to a number of refinements and new techniques in Army aviation maintenance and support. The aircraft depot maintenance ship *Corpus Christi Bay*, deployed in 1966, continued to support Army aircraft in Vietnam by overhauling and repairing engines and components and by fabricating parts required for grounded aircraft as well as other equipment. The ship moved up and down the coast to provide maintenance close to operating aviation units.

The Aviation Closed Loop Support Program managed aircraft and supporting engines, components, and ancillary equipment through a full cycle, sending serviceable equipment to the field and returning unserviceable items from the field to the continental United States for overhaul and repair. The effectiveness of the over-all logistic system is measured by the fact that the Army has been able to support over 4,000 aircraft in Vietnam with the highest operational readiness and utilization rates ever achieved.

The integration of systems management procurement and overhaul programs has improved control over aircraft engines and other high dollar value components. In the last year a supply of spare engines and components with an acquisition value of about $136 million was identified that, when overhauled, may be installed in new aircraft at about 18 percent of the acquisition value when new.

Experience in Vietnam also led to a weapon systems management concept for Army aircraft under which an aircraft is treated as a complete piece of equipment, including avionics, armament, and supporting materiel. The techniques of weapons systems management are being extended worldwide without compromising either the over-all logistic system or the command management structure. The aviation logistic program in Europe was reviewed by Headquarters, U.S. Army, Europe, and the Department of the Army during the year, leading to some changes which take advantage of Vietnam experience and will improve logistic support.

Supply and Depot Management

The Department of the Army Distribution-Allocation Committee (DADAC), the agency that controls the distribution of certain items actually or potentially in short supply, continued to regulate well over 200 items during the fiscal year. The DADAC functions during periods of logistical turbulence when normal supply procedures and priority systems cannot be applied uniformily for selected items.

Major item distribution plans (MIDP) have been developed over the past three years to provide the departmental headquarters and major commanders with an efficient and effective mechanism to manage major equipment items. These plans reflect worldwide requirements for an item; display the assets on hand against the requirements; and show the planned receipts, losses, diversions, returns, requirements changes, and distribution for a two-year period. The major item distribution plans will be used to determine the Army's logistical capability to support unit reorganizations and war plans, forecast the allocation of future stocks, and determine if redistribution of stock from lower to higher priority claimants is justified. As of June 30, 1970, MIDP preparation was automated for all commodity areas except aircraft and missiles.

The Army Stock Fund finances much of the materiel that flows through the depot system. Stock Fund purchase authority in fiscal year 1970 amounted to $2.9 billion, about 20 percent less than in 1969, while the issue program was $3.6 billion, about 8 percent below the previous year. Because of the decline in demand, stockages were reduced at depot level. Technological advances, such as faster transportation, improved containerization, better movement control, and automated management systems that improve stock control, have enabled the Army to reduce stocks at all supply echelons.

The Defense Integrated Management Engineering Systems

(DIMES) was being implemented in Army warehousing and inventory control activities worldwide as the year closed. Man-hour, work load, and performance data for these activities became available to management at all levels from depots and inventory control points to the departmental headquarters and the Office of the Secretary of Defense, to be used for production planning and control and for manpower management and budgetary purposes at all levels. Integration of the Department of Defense Warehousing Gross Performance Measurement System into DIMES was completed as the year closed, as was a test of DIMES in Army Materiel Command and U.S. Army, Europe, inventory control points.

Modernization of the depot storage system in the United States began in fiscal year 1967 as part of a $14.7 million three-year program to equip depots with the most efficient materiel handling systems and provide modern facilities, design capabilities, and layouts for effective storage operations. Through fiscal year 1970, $9.9 million had been spent on procurement of handling equipment and alterations to facilities, while $2.3 million was obligated for military construction under the program. These expenditures saved 227 personnel spaces ($1.3 million in annual operating costs). When the modernization program is completed, depot storage operating costs are expected to be reduced by $3.9 million annually (524 personnel spaces).

Depot organization as well as modernization was a subject of attention in the fiscal year. In May 1969, a revised depot organization regulation was issued to assist depot commanders around the world to establish and maintain a uniform structure. The standard organization makes more effective use of resources and takes advantage of the latest organizational experience of the Army. The advantages to be obtained through uniformity are evident in some simple statistics: there were 49 Army depots, 38 depot activities, and 17 miscellaneous activities with a storage mission in nine countries (United States, Japan, Korea, Okinawa, Thailand, Vietnam, United Kingdom, Germany, and Italy) on December 31, 1969, storing some six million short tons of Army supplies and equipment and performing such wholesale functions as storage and warehousing, repair and rebuild, rail and motor vehicle traffic management, stock control, overhead and support functions, quality control, and property disposal, among other depot and tenant activities. Additionally, action was initiated to create a theater-oriented depot complex, to focus support efforts on U.S. Army, Europe, as a part of accelerated direct supply support to improve response time in meeting theater Army supply requirements.

During fiscal year 1969 the Joint Logistics Review Board began to revise the management procedures under which petroleum products are distributed to Army units throughout the world. Terminal reporting and inventory accounting were standardized and procedures for computation of reserves were revised to include reappraisal of consumption factors. Since commercial distribution facilities are used as much as possible, accounting procedures were revised to make civilian and military distribution systems compatible.

Transportation

In fiscal year 1970 the volume of Army cargo and the number of Army passengers moved varied slightly from the previous year. The Military Sea Transportation Service moved about 97 percent of the cargo that was shipped, that is, 16,015,400 measurement tons, about 2,886,200 less than the 1969 volume. The 227,045 short tons that the Army shipped by air was also under the figure for 1969.

Passenger movements continued to reflect the policy of using the most expeditious means to move personnel and save man-days of travel. During the year 1,673,300 Army-sponsored passengers were transported worldwide, 1,573,400 by air and 99,900 by sea. The ratio of passengers using airlift decreased along with the number of passengers moved.

A curb on the use of premium transportation was maintained through the year under the Airlift Challenge Program, which provides for automatic review, screening, and challenge of requests from field commands. An average of 3,400 shipments per month was diverted from airlift to sealift at an estimated savings of about $11.5 million per month. These diversions were without detriment to delivery dates.

Military Standard Transportation and Movement Procedures, the so-called MILSTAMP program, continued during the report period to provide a reliable standardized method for movement and documentation of cargo within the Defense Transportation System. To improve co-ordinated transportation and supply planning, a logistics intelligence file was established at the Army's Logistics Control Office, Pacific, enhancing automated management control over the materiel pipeline to Vietnam. This file is activated when a requisition is placed on a continental U.S. supply source; the file is updated to reflect each subsequent transaction along the supply and transportation path to arrival at the water terminal. Information is readily available on quantities and tonnages.

The Army's move into the field of container system operations met with some difficulty during the year. A contract for 2,000 containers (to be called MILVANs), negotiated with Baifield Industries of Dallas, Texas, in November 1968, failed to produce containers in the quantity and of the quality desired. The 224 containers delivered between May and September 1969 were only conditionally acceptable, and at mid-September, when all were deadlined for defects in workmanship and design, the contract was terminated for default. As the fiscal year closed, bids had been received for a new contract and preaward investigations were in progress. Meanwhile, deliveries of container chassis, also contracted in November 1968, were on schedule.

To launch the MILVAN pilot operation at the earliest possible date, the Army Materiel Command sought and was granted funds to lease 1,300 containers 8'x8'x20' in size. Contracts were signed with two container lessors in April 1970, and the Army arranged with the Military Sea Transportation Service to provide sealift between the west coast and Vietnam. The first ship departed the Military Ocean Terminal, Bay Area, in California on June 9, 1970. Subsequent sailings were scheduled at fifteen-day intervals.

The Mobility Equipment Research and Development Center at Fort Belvoir, Virginia, has prototypes of a number of items of equipment under consideration for future Army containerization systems. The Combat Developments Command was asked to study the problem of discharge of non-self-sustaining container transport systems.

To support current and future over-the-shore operations—a critical link in the logistical chain—a research, development, testing, and procurement program must be established to equip Army elements with modern lighterage that is compatible with the latest concepts in commercial shipping. The Army Materiel Command was conducting a study to identify deficiencies in the present fleet and to develop information required to modernize it. The Combat Developments Command, meanwhile, was studying lighterage requirements for the 1975–85 period.

Although the Army is the land element of U.S. military forces, water is often an obstacle to ground operations and the Army has always required organic marine craft and equipment to cross or surmount water obstacles in carrying out its mission. The roles and missions that might be assigned to transhydro craft in the 1975–85 decade have been under study. The term "transhydro" includes craft that float on the surface, those supported by air cushion or foils, and those that fly over water.

A number of factors have given some urgency to such a study. A significant portion of the Army's marine fleet is wearing out, while bloc obsolescence is overtaking many models of Army floating craft. It has been necessary to depend on the Navy to provide waterborne tactical mobility. Doctrinal and organizational literature has been both inadequate and inconsistent; many functions and missions have been assigned to Army floating craft units in Vietnam. New concepts as well as types of equipment have been developed to perform transhydro roles and missions. Thus the Combat Developments Command developed a study plan in this field and preliminary efforts began in the last quarter of the fiscal year.

The extensive requirement for lighterage in Southeast Asia to support tactical and logistical operations practically depleted depot stocks of landing craft. To meet the requirements, all LCM–8's and LCU's prepositioned in Europe were withdrawn and shipped to Vietnam. Except for forty LCM–8's, the landing craft in the Army system were procured in 1950–52 and are now reaching an age when repair and spare parts support are difficult. Landing craft have had wide and hard use in Vietnam, reducing their economical life expectancy. Present procurement includes only sixty-one LCM–8's.

Containerized shipment of ammunition was tested during the last fiscal year. Some 226 containers were loaded with military explosives at four inland production plants and one depot. The containers were moved by highway to the Naval Weapons Station at Concord, California, where they were loaded aboard a crane-equipped container ship, transported to Cam Ranh Bay in Vietnam, offloaded, and moved by a combination of coastal vessel and highway to Ban Me Thuot, Qui Nhon, Pleiku, and Landing Zone English. No intermediate handling of the ammunition was required between the production plant and the Vietnam destination.

Participating in this test were the Army Materiel Command and the Military Traffic Management and Terminal Service. Because the test was a one-time operation to be completed at an early date, certain adverse features were unavoidable. For example, moving loaded containers to the west coast by road instead of rail increased land movement costs considerably. The combination of a large container and a 75-percent safety limit on the lifting crane resulted in a low cube utilization of the container. Blocking and bracing standards imposed by the U.S. Coast Guard resulted in a complex blocking arrangement that was costly to install and remove and added significantly to gross weight. Furthermore, the one-time test did not allow negotiators to offer continuing shipments to highway and ocean carriers, which meant higher costs for one-time transportation.

Operationally the test demonstrated that real benefits could be attained through the shipment of containerized ammunition. Vessel turnaround was improved by 500 percent over break-bulk handling. Manpower efficiency was increased by 600 percent. These improvements promise a significant increase in the port throughput (berth and anchor discharge, onward movement, destination reception) capacity over that achieved in break-bulk handling. Increased manpower work loads at points of origin and destination were more than offset by over-all savings. The number of handlings was reduced from a possible eight by break-bulk to only two. The ammunition was in better condition on delivery, and lot integrity was preserved. The reduction in pipeline time would foster pipeline inventory savings when containerized shipments were routine. As fiscal year 1970 closed, actions were being taken to develop a total system for the containerized shipment of ammunition.

To protect national interests, Public Law 90–500 of 1969 restricted the acquisition of foreign-manufactured buses, either by purchase, rental, or transportation services contract. To comply with the law, foreign-leased buses were to be replaced. The program schedules replacement of 100 buses in Korea from 1968 procurement and 250 in Thailand, Japan, and Okinawa from 1969 procurement. Another 519 buses are to be procured in the United States with fiscal year 1970 funds.

Logistic Improvements in Supply, Maintenance, and Transportation Operations

A wide range of management techniques have been developed to "do more with less and do it better," which resulted in estimated cost benefits of over $2 billion. Costly and critical items have been brought under more visible control; weapons system management has been intensified; maintenance and repair cycles have been formalized and emphasized; and direct exchange practices have been expanded. All of these procedures help insure that the right amount is at the right place at the right time. One of the more significant facets of the logistics offensive referred to earlier is inventory in motion. This is a supply management program that works to lower stock levels at immobile depots in the combat zone. Integrated supply and transportation planning, real time control of in-transit stocks, and more intensive management will accelerate resupply, lower inventory levels, and reduce requirements for static stocks on the ground.

Early in the fiscal year the Army was faced with the challenge of improving logistic efficiency and readiness worldwide within current and projected reductions in manpower, money, and materiel. The primary concern was how, in the face of reductions, the Army would continue to carry out logistic functions and support services efficiently and effectively, so that combat forces would continue to be supported adequately.

The major commands and oversea theaters dramatized the problem in the logistic operations STREAMLINE, considering reductions in materiel procurement authorization, operating funds, and personnel; improved logistic management and operations concepts and techniques that would capitalize on advancing technology in military equipment; and communications. The concept addresses all facets of logistics concurrently and includes the elimination of unnecessary stock and echelons of supply, the improvement of transportation capabilities including containerization, and the modification of maintenance procedures to permit more maintenance at less cost. The program was initiated in U.S. Army, Pacific, in the third quarter of fiscal year 1970 and will be executed in other commands in fiscal year 1971.

As a part of the logistic offensive, stockage policies for support activities of the Army in the field were modified. The number of items to be stocked below the continental U.S. depot level were reduced from 1,063,000 federal stock numbers on July 1, 1969, to 509,000 on June 30, 1970. Goals were established for the number that can be on a stockage list. The aim is to reduce inventory investment by eliminating stockage of slow-moving items below depot level. Since fewer items would be stocked, management would be improved. More economical ordering will reduce requisitions and transaction volume both in administration and handling.

Excess supply levels have been created worldwide as a result of force reductions and logistic improvements. Thus Project Clean was established in November 1969 to weed excess materiel from the entire Army supply system, to identify and redistribute it within the Army and to other Department of Defense agencies where possible, and to dispose of unneeded supplies. Departmental teams visited oversea commands to provide on-the-spot disposition instructions for excess materiel.

A major constraint in the rapid disposition of excess materiel has been the long screening time required by current regulations. To reduce the screening cycle, it was proposed under the project for utilization and redistribution of materiel (PURM) in the Pacific area that present sequential screenings through a variety of agencies be made concurrently. This procedure will begin in October 1970.

Under the aegis of this program, special attention was given to the supply posture in Vietnam. With the gradual lessening of the conflict, a troop withdrawal in progress, the gradual assumption of battlefield responsibility by the Vietnamese, and eventual American withdrawal in prospect, stock levels could be lowered and the wastage that followed the termination of several past wars avoided. Review of the supply stockage in Vietnam indicates that, during fiscal year 1970, levels were reduced by over 250,000 short tons valued at over half a billion dollars. This reduction was accomplished by a combination of limiting requisitions for supplies for U.S. and Free World forces to careful levels; by normal attrition; by redistributing materiel in the country; and by withdrawing some stocks from Vietnam. Additionally, Project Stop and See provided for the cancellation of requisitions for items valued at $221 million which were already in sufficient supply in Vietnam or which would overburden the storage capability there.

Also during the fiscal year, 75,500 short tons of materiel valued at $158.5 million were withdrawn from Vietnam and sent to bases in Japan and Okinawa, while another 137,000 short tons of both serviceable and unserviceable but repairable materiel, valued at $870 million, were shipped to the United States for return to stock or for repair and return to use. Planning envisions ending fiscal year 1971 with no significant excess materiel in U.S. Army, Vietnam, depots.

As the year closed, the departmental headquarters had developed procedures for testing, beginning in July 1970, a direct support system that would involve a theater-oriented depot complex in the United States and the 3d Infantry and 4th Armored Divisions in Europe. The system is expected to reduce the present order and ship time—approximately ninety-five days from continental U.S. supply sources through U.S. Army, Europe (USAREUR), depots to the direct support unit of the divisions—to thirty-five days from the continental United States. Operation of the system with these divisions will be compared with supply operations of the other divisions in Europe, and should the test prove effective, the direct support system will be expanded to all USAREUR direct support units. In general, the new system will permit static storage on the ground to be reduced by the amount in transit; reveal when, where, and how stocks will arrive; eliminate multiple handling; curtail pilferage; and reduce inventories.

Along similar lines, a concept was developed and agreed upon in April 1970 for a pilot project under which commissaries in Europe would be supported by direct deliveries. The Defense Personnel Support Center would receive requisitions from six commissaries, presently supported by the depot at Giessen, Germany, consolidate requirements by item, procure the goods at its Philadelphia depot, and prepare and ship direct to the commissaries in Europe. The program would reduce inventory and investment in pipeline supplies; reduce brand name resale functions at the Giessen depot; improve customer service; and supply fresher products. If the pilot program proves successful, the system will be extended worldwide.

A logistic system that operates worldwide using every mode of transportation to serve a million and a half people with products and services is inherently complex and requires a library of printed rules and regulations to operate effectively. Both the Department of the Army's board of inquiry on the Army logistic system and its inspector general inquiry into Army regulations and related publications in 1967 concluded that from the user's point of view most regulations were hard to read and understand. The practice of promulgating policies and procedures in small, topically oriented directives, while easier for the author, usually resulted in excessive cross-referencing, needless repetition, and conflicts between separate regulations. On the other hand, they cited as good, usable regulations those that consolidated a number of previous regulations into the single, more self-contained type of directive.

In line with this philosophy, corrective action was begun in July 1969 to consolidate 128 existing Army regulations on logistics into 14 comprehensive ones. As the work progressed, outdated regulations received badly needed attention. By the close of the year one of the fourteen regulations had been completed and three were being edited. The remainder will be completed in fiscal year 1971.

Under study during the year was a proposal that airlift be used as a routine method of delivery for selected commodities, if use of air produced over-all economies in the pipeline. Under this procedure, the increased cost of airlift would be offset by savings in procurement, reduction in stock levels, and improved supply control. Commodities were being reviewed to identify eligible items for the airlift program. Through Research Analysis Corporation investigations and the C–5A Heavy Lift Aircraft Study, selection techniques and formulas were being developed based on pipeline savings and holdings, transportation, and packaging cost differentials.

The Army's requirement for logistic readiness has the same consistency and importance as the nation's requirement for the Army as an instrument of national security. However, the omnipresent competition for resources makes the Army's fulfillment of that requirement a challenge under the best of conditions and a most difficult task during periods of declining resources and increasing budgetary constraints. Therefore, in the effort to insure fulfillment of its responsibilities in the area of logistic readiness, the Army developed intensive management techniques to monitor readiness, detect and correct problems in their early stages, and insure that the logistic system is responsive to valid command requirements. These special techniques were employed through intensive management programs in U.S. Army, Europe; Continental Army Command; Eighth U.S. Army; and U.S. Army, Alaska, and applied to those units and resources where the most critical logistics readiness problems were being encountered.

During fiscal year 1970, these programs contributed to achievement of the highest level of logistic readiness on a worldwide basis that had been possible since U.S. Army direct involvement in Southeast Asia (1965).

Logistic Doctrine and Systems

Installation of a division logistic system continued during the report year. The system is designed to standardize the logistic systems in divisions by automating functional tasks; to improve the compatibility of division and supporting installation logistic systems; to improve the quality and flow of logistic data; to simplify division logistic procedures for soldiers with limited service; and to promote a smooth transition to future automated logistic systems. It provides for automatic property books and equipment and status reporting, establishing a central issue facility, automating the division's class IX repair parts system, reorganizing the supply office, and establishing a division data center.

The Supply and Maintenance Plan and Report, an improved control system developed for supply and maintenance activities financed from the Army's operations and maintenance appropriations, has been successfully tested in supply operations and is being extended to other program elements. The system, which isolates key performance indicators and brings together work load, manpower, and financial data, is designed to serve operational, manpower, and financial managers. The Army Materiel Command prototype will be completed in fiscal year 1971 and Army-wide implementation is planned for fiscal year 1972.

During the past year the Army developed its concept and policy for use of the Air Force C–5A Galaxy and other heavy lift aircraft, such as the C–141 Starlifter and the Boeing 747 of the Civilian Reserve Air Fleet, in the resupply role. To satisfy the Army concepts, a series of actions to correct specific deficiencies or voids in existing logistic systems have been assigned to selected Army elements. This running level of preparedness will permit logistic structure modifications to accommodate increasing air lift capabilities.

Historically, the methods by which supplies and services are procured and supplied to the field have been developed through logistic systems operated independently by various Army command echelons. To achieve centralized control over system developments in order to eliminate duplication, and to reduce costs, a project called Turn the Corner was launched in December 1969 that would make full use of automation and associated communications networks. It is the first step in establishing vertical control over logistic system development. Under the project, a common baseline of logistic requirements will be established. Existing operating systems will be examined and analyzed against the baseline and brought into alignment.

Looking even further into the future, an ad hoc review and analysis group was convened in November 1969 to establish the concept, principles, and objectives for a readiness-oriented logistic system for 1975 and beyond. The group examined the requirements for changes in logistic doctrine and for new subsystems or changes to existing ones. Its report was included in the master planning in progress at the U.S. Army Logistics Doctrine, Systems, and Readiness Agency at the New Cumberland Army Depot in Harrisburg, Pennsylvania.

As the year closed the first phase of a new selected item management system (SIMS) was ready to go into operation to improve control over about 4,000 high value items, both reparables and consumables. This system will be expanded eventually to some 26,000 items representing 80 percent of dollar procurement and 80 percent of demand. SIMS will ultimately eliminate the need for separate reporting systems, by establishing one standard system. It is anticipated that the system will enhance the readiness of units around the world, permit reduction of inventories, reduce procurement actions, and utilize stocks to the maximum through repair and return to stock.

The five-year automatic data processing program being conducted by the Army Materiel Command to develop standard systems that would operate on standard equipment with standard computer programs and software moved ahead during the year. Destined for commodity commands and national inventory control points, depots, arsenals, laboratories, test and evaluation activities, and data banks, it will be applied by activity beginning in the fall of 1970.

Facilities and Construction

The 1970 Military Construction Authorization Act approved on December 5, 1969, provided $280 million in new funding authorization for the Army. An additional $12.7 million had already been approved in November under Public Law 91–121 for research, development, test, and evaluation facilities at the Kwajalein Missile Range. A fiscal year 1970 military construction appropriation of $287.2 million in new obligational authority was approved in December 1969.

The Army in fiscal year 1970 thus had available for military construction a total of $932 million, exclusive of $248,250 transferred to the General Services Administration (GSA) for office rental; $287 million in current appropriations; $622.6 million in unobligated carryover from prior-year appropriations; $12.1 million transferred from Secretary of Defense contingency funds; $1 million for the civilian pay raise; and $9.3 million derived from recoupments in the infrastructure program. The funds for new work were available as follows (in millions of dollars) :

Major projects (excluding Vietnam, Thailand, and Safeguard)	370.1
Vietnam and Thailand	168.3
Safeguard (including planning)	293.9
Infrastructure	52.9
General authorization	46.8
Total	932.0

The delay in congressional action on the fiscal year 1970 appropriation bill limited construction starts during the first half to projects authorized and funded in prior years. In addition, the President on September 4, 1969, directed all agencies of the federal government to reduce contracts for government construction by 75 percent in an effort to east inflationary pressures in the construction industry. Under Bureau of the Budget guidelines issued September 12, 1969, the following categories were excluded from the base program subject to the 75 percent deferral requirement: land acquisition, planning and design, access roads, Vietnam construction in the country, obligations for local labor and materials or use of foreign currencies for oversea projects, urgent national security requirements, and restoration of facilities damaged or destroyed by fire, flood, or other natural disasters. The approved Department of Defense program permitted the Army to obligate $82.9 million for Army military construction projects, $15.7 million for family housing, and $2.3 million for Army Reserve construction. The Bureau of the Budget, in subsequent actions, released all pollution abatement and family housing projects which were ready for award, and advised that effective July 1, 1970, the direct federal construction deferral would be replaced by the requirement that executive departments and agencies proceed with construction projects in their 1971 budget plans on a selective basis if and as necessary to avoid aggravating congested inflationary conditions in local construction market areas.

Despite these restrictions, the Army made major progress in reducing unobligated balances from $622.6 million at the end of fiscal year 1966 to $409 million on June 30, 1970. Obligations for major projects totaled $172.8 million in areas outside of Vietnam and Thailand, excluding Safeguard. Some $100.1 million was obligated for new work in Vietnam and Thailand, while $197.1 million was obligated for Safeguard, $28.2 million for infrastructure, and $24.8 million for planning, minor construction, and access roads. Major contributions to support worldwide Army operations included the start of construction to support Safeguard deployment.

Construction awards for improving and updating industrial facilities at government-owned plants totaled approximately an additional $125.4 million. During the year, fifty-two projects were completed at a cost of $70.7 million.

At the beginning of fiscal year 1970, there was $113.9 million of unobligated funds and $54.4 million of unapportioned funds available for construction in Southeast Asia. Due to the availability of these funds and the decision to limit the type of projects on which new starts would be initiated, it was decided not to request additional construction funds in the fiscal year 1970 program for support of Southeast Asia operations. By the end of fiscal year 1970, the unobligated balance had been reduced to $68.2 million including unapportioned funds of $34.2 million. Over $1.3 billion in regular, contingency, and military assistance funds have been applied to military construction in support of Southeast Asia operations during fiscal years 1965–70.

The Army's military construction program consists of three basic elements: providing facilities that installations need but do not have; replacing aged and obsolete facilities; and improving and modernizing existing facilities. Based upon an assumed long-range permanent Army peacetime strength of 925,000, there is a facilities deficit of about $7.5 billion (excluding Safeguard construction). It was the Army's objective to invest $800 million in construction funds annually to overcome the deficit in about ten years. However, projected budget limitations will allow only a $325 million annual investment for facilities, possibly making' it necessary to extend this objective an additional ten years. The $100 million authorized and funded by Congress in fiscal year 1970 for replacement and modernization is indicative of the restraints placed on the amount of new construction to be undertaken until the war in Southeast Asia is ended.

On October 29, 1969, and again on March 6, 1970, the Secretary of Defense announced actions to consolidate, reduce, realign, or close various defense installations in the United States. The major actions which have been completed or which are under way are the disposal of the Army Pictorial Center, Long Island, New York, and of major portions of the Granite City Army Depot in Illinois and Fort Holabird in Maryland, and the inactivation of Fort Irwin in California. Additionally, both the Navajo Army Depot in Arizona and the Fort Wingate Army Depot in New Mexico will be stocked with war reserve ammunition and placed in a standby status. The Army will also dispose of the majority of the Military Ocean Terminal, Kings Bay, Georgia. Included in the action were reductions in authorized base operating strengths and in numerous Army installations worldwide.

Expenditures for real property maintenance activities at Army installations in fiscal year 1970 were slightly over $1 billion, approximately equal to expenditures for the previous fiscal year. Army building space decreased by over 800,000 square feet, or less than 1 percent of the previous fiscal year's total, as a result of the discontinuance of some facilities. Unfinanced real property maintenance and repair at the end of the fiscal year was approximately $385 million, an increase of about 15 percent over the previous fiscal year.

Real property maintenance in Southeast Asia was done primarily by contractors. In Vietnam, one firm with a work force of about 21,000 furnished all normal facilities engineering support to about 500,000 U.S. Army and allied assistance personnel at 105 locations. The same firm, with a force of about 2,400, provided the same type of services to U.S. Army forces in Thailand. Another contractor operated and maintained high voltage electric generation plants and their distribution systems, including four steam floating barge sites and two diesel land-based sites in Vietnam.

The Army, through the Corps of Engineers, provided construction support to numerous agencies and projects, among them the Air Force (including its National Guard and Reserve), the Navy, the National Aeronautics and Space Administration, various Department of Defense agencies, the Agency for International Development, the U.S. Information Agency, the trust territory of the Pacific islands, the Robert F. Kennedy gravesite, national cemeteries, and selected foreign governments. During the fiscal year 1970, Army Engineers contracted for approximately $142 million of construction for these other U.S. agencies and foreign governments. In December 1967 the Secretary of the Army was assigned responsibility for the Homeowners Assistance Program, under which military or civilian employees of Department of Defense activities are given financial assistance to reduce their losses if they are required to dispose of a home when a military installation is closed. Through June 30, 1970, 7,892 applications for assistance had been received and 4,592 applicants had been given financial assistance totaling $11,589,000. Over 1,100 mortgages totaling $8,589,000 were assumed, while 1,904 applications were rejected.

Standard engineering designs for the major tactical Safeguard facilities were completed and adapted for the sites in the vicinity of Grand Forks, North Dakota. Construction of the major tactical facilities at both of the North Dakota sites began under a $138 million contract awarded on March 31, 1970. Construction also started at both of the sites in the vicinity of Great Falls, Montana, under preliminary contracts pending completion of engineering design for these sites. The major construction contracts for the Montana sites were to be awarded during fiscal year 1971.

The 1970 Military Construction Appropriation Act, approved in December 1969, provided $287.2 million in new obligational authority for the Army. Congress approved a total obligational authority of $410.1 million with $100.9 million to be financed from prior-year unobligated balances; however a general reduction of $22 million was imposed, bringing the Army's fiscal year 1970 military construction appropriation to $287.2 million. The $22 million reduction, made without reference to specific projects, required the Army to defer certain items which are considered to be urgently required.

To deploy Exercise Reforger units rapidly and achieve a high level of combat readiness almost simultaneously with their arrival in Europe, unit equipment must be prepositioned on the European continent and maintained in a high state of readiness. An essential element in the ability to attain such a state of equipment readiness, as well as in facilitating the rapid issue of equipment to Reforger units on arrival in the theater, is controlled humidity storage. Present plans call for the storage of all Reforger prepositioned equipment in controlled humidity warehouses.

In the first quarter of fiscal year 1970 a plan was approved by the Department of the Army to establish a line of communications for wartime emergency support of U.S. forces in central Europe.

The purpose of this action is to replace the capability sacrificed by the withdrawal of U.S. forces from France. In addition, steps were initiated to realign the peacetime line of communications in support of U.S. Army, Europe. The dependence upon the port of Bremerhaven in Germany was being reduced through its combined use with Belgian and Dutch ports. The combined costs of cargo handling and onward movement influenced port selection and made it possible to reduce support operations in the Bremerhaven area and achieve maximum economies in cargo transportation operations.

Under the military construction program, the Army continued to fund the U.S. share of the NATO Common Infrastructure Program. The Congress authorized and appropriated the $50 million budget request. The other NATO nations agreed to share the cost of relocating U.S. facilities from France, and reimbursements began in the fourth quarter of the fiscal year.

The Military Liquidation Section, established on February 1, 1967, to dispose of U.S. installations and other interests in France, was phased out and inactivated on June 30, 1970. During this period the section released 386 U.S. installations to the government of France. The United States acquired $21.2 million as proceeds from the sale of U.S. real and related personal property and from the rental of surplus commodity housing. Responsibility for the disposal of four remaining surplus commodity housing areas in France has been assigned to U.S. Army, Europe.

Support Services

The Army continued to administer eighty-five national cemeteries during the year. The proposal that the National Cemetery System be transferred to the Veterans Administration, under consideration for several years and reintroduced when the 91st Congress convened in January 1969, was not acted upon. During fiscal year 1970, a total of 38,028 interments were made in the eighty-five cemeteries, 1,198 of them Vietnam casualties interred in sixty-two cemeteries. Fifty of the cemeteries had gravesites available at year's end, while thirty-five others had gravesites available only for Vietnam casualties or for second interments under the single gravesite policy. A total of 200,445 grave markers were furnished to national and private cemeteries.

The Army operated ten mortuaries overseas and one at the Oakland Army Terminal in California, providing mortuary service for 10,306 deceased military personnel, dependents, and other eligible categories for whom the service is authorized. In the continental United States, funeral homes, through contract arrangement with military installations, provided mortuary service for 2,093 deceased.

The bodies of seven World War II and Korean War dead were recovered and identified in the last year from Germany, Holland, Korea, and New Guinea. Army representatives visited the next of kin in each case to report the recovery circumstances and identification procedures.

Army mortuary teams were employed on an emergency basis during the Hurricane Camille disaster on the gulf coast, when regional establishments were unable to cope with the situation.

An important element of the Army's responsibility to deceased personnel and their families is the processing of personal effects. In Vietnam a personal property depot receives property from units and mortuaries, corresponds with the next of kin, and ships the personal effects to the person eligible to take custody. In other areas of the world, summary courts are appointed to carry out this responsibility.

During the fiscal year, excess, surplus, and foreign excess personal property with an acquisition cost of $1,293 million was turned over to Army property disposal activities for disposition by redistribution or transfer, donation, sale, or other authorized disposal action. Usable property with an acquisition cost of $340 million and 383,000 short tons of scrap were sold. Proceeds amounted to $52 million; the cost of operating the disposal program was $31 million.

Inventories of usable property for disposal increased during the year from $502 million to $564 million. The major causes of the increase were returns from Southeast Asia, increased efforts to remove unneeded or obsolete items from the supply system, and a phasing down of activities and installations. Increased emphasis was placed on disposal activities, and plans were being developed to simplify and streamline the disposal process.

Military Assistance

The materiel portion of the 1970 Army Military Assistance Program (MAP) totaled $337 million and included varying degrees of support for countries and international organizations. Grant aid recipients received $222 million in materiel, for which the Army was reimbursed, and $296 million without reimbursement during the fiscal year. Materiel delivered was predominantly from prior-year undelivered balances or from Army excess.

In addition, aid to Thailand and Laos continued to require

increased attention as a result of the conflict in Vietnam. During fiscal year 1970, $152 million in materiel orders were received for Thailand and Laos, and deliveries of $90 million were made.

Continuous surveillance and close scrutiny have been applied to limit to the absolute minimum the gold flow resulting from the grant aid program. Foreign currencies instead of U.S. dollars were used wherever possible; offshore procurement was reduced; and oversea travel was curtailed. In this connection, the aid mission assigned to U.S. Army, Japan, was eliminated during the year.

During the year the Army continued to transfer to the Military Assistance Program, at no cost, materiel that was in long supply or excess to needs. This program was initiated during fiscal year 1969, and refined and expanded during fiscal year 1970. During the year, materiel with an acquisition value of $229 million was transferred to the Military Assistance Program and $2 million in Laos and Thailand under this program. In furtherance of MAP objectives, the program encourages recipients to accept major items of materiel "as-is" with rehabilitation and shipping expenses being assumed by the recipient. Principal recipients of materiel under this program were the Republic of China, Korea, Turkey, and Greece.

With the spread of the Vietnamese conflict throughout Indochina, aid to Laos, Thailand, and Cambodia became increasingly important. During the year M16 rifles, armored cars, and communications equipment were furnished to Laos to modernize its forces. Thailand received M16 rifles, vehicles, construction equipment, and communications equipment. Military aid to Cambodia resumed during 1970 for the first time since fiscal year 1964. The extent and content of this aid was modest and rather limited as the year closed.

Through a combination grant-aid military sales agreement, equipment for an additional air defense (Nike) unit was being supplied to the Republic of China. A large portion of this materiel was being made available from Army excesses under the program described above; therefore, no reimbursement from MAP funds will be required. To improve Korean mobility and counterinsurgency capabilities, the shipment of equipment for an additional helicopter company was completed during the year. Helicopters were also supplied to the Philippines to provide much needed mobility.

During the year the Army actively participated in negotiations covering military assistance aspects of the extension of the Spanish Base Rights Agreement.

To further the MAP objective of making recipient countries self-supporting by building up their economy and industry, military aid to nations achieving a satisfactory state of economic development was being discontinued. As part of this objective, the MAP materiel program for Iran was discontinued in fiscal year 1970.

During the fiscal year, the Army sold materiel and services valued at $319.1 million to fifty-four countries and five international organizations under the auspices of the foreign military sales program. In the conduct of its sales activities, the Army adhered to the policy that materiel readily available through commercial sources would be sold directly by U.S. industry to the recipient. Through intensive management procedures 1,590 outstanding sales cases were balanced and closed out in supply records.

The Army's Logistical Orientation Tour Program brought seven groups of high-ranking military personnel from seven countries to the United States during the fiscal year to acquaint them with new military systems and equipment of mutual interest in Free World defense. A demonstration of the M–561 (Gama Goat) vehicle was conducted in Europe for members of the NATO community. Similarly, briefings were given to representatives of these same countries on the Redeye weapons system, TACFIRE (an automated system for artillery fire control), and modernization of the Nike-Hercules missile system.

During the fiscal year, the Army participated in seventeen coproduction programs with six foreign nations and one international organization, NATO. Under this program, and based on a government-to-government agreement, a foreign nation may assemble or manufacture major end items or weapons systems of U.S. origin. The programs are valued at $1,482.2 million with expenditures for goods and services in the United States valued at $556.2 million. Participating countries are the Federal Republic of Germany, Italy, the Netherlands, Norway, Japan, and the Republic of China. Items of U.S. origin being coproduced include the M–113 armored personnel carrier family of vehicles, the M–60 tank, the UH–1D and UH–1H helicopters, the Nike-Hawk missile, the M109 self-propelled howitzer, wheeled vehicles, a light antitank weapon, and small arms.

Under the auspices of co-operative logistics, the Army maintained supply support arrangements with seventeen foreign countries and one international organization, NATO. These programs provide participating countries with continuous follow-on support for major end items and weapons systems of U.S. origin on a reimbursable basis. This program was valued at $158 million during the fiscal year and involved the support of a variety of items such as conventional weapons, vehicles, Sergeant, Pershing, and Hawk.

International logistic management activities were substantially expanded during the fiscal year. Within those management improvements initiated in prior fiscal years, Department of the Army objectives were established on a progressive basis which would further strengthen the management and overview of each area.

In response to numerous requests from Military Assistance Advisory Groups and foreign country representatives, named-ship manifests were developed which would provide specific detailed information of the materiel loaded on each ship, for which the recipient country would then plan for offloading and receipt. This manifest is provided for grant aid recipients and select sales countries. It is airmailed immediately following the loading of each vessel, and has proven to be a most useful tool.

Time frames were established for international logistic billing actions in previous fiscal years. During this fiscal year, intense management in this area resulted in marked improvements; bills were being processed within the appropriate period. Army operating and capital accounts were thus receiving reimbursement on a timely basis.

Support to foreign countries improved during the fiscal year, and extensive progress was made by all national inventory control points. The support of international logistics was accorded a high priority, and performance improved accordingly. A program of tight control was initiated and the fill rate improved. Concurrent with the increased fill rate there was a reduction in back orders. A system of control and validation was established for both major items and repair parts, which will insure continued high performance.

IX. Research and Development

The Army conducts both basic and applied research. In fiscal year 1970, the commitment in Southeast Asia gave direction to much of the research effort, but long-range projects also retained a share of the funding.

In fiscal year 1970, the Army's approved research and development program totaled $1,631.9 million, some $30 million less than the figure for fiscal year 1969.

A restrictive clause of the 1970 Defense Appropriation Act (Public Law 91–171) stated that funds for research, development, evaluation, or testing, when unobligated for periods longer than two years, should be proposed for recission. To insure maximum use of available resources, the Army established a recoupment objective of $33 million from unobligated balances to fund high priority fiscal year 1970 requirements. The Army was able to recoup $28.8 million and submitted formal requests for approval to reprogram $24.4 million. By June 30, 1970, the Congress had approved reprograming of $12 million to finance civilian pay raises. Other actions were withdrawn by the Army for further consideration.

During fiscal year 1970, it was necessary to obtain additional emergency funds for accelerated research and development in support of Southeast Asia operations. Of the $34.1 million in emergency funds requested, the Office of the Secretary of Defense released $23.3 million.

On June 30, 1970, the $1,631.9 million allocation for Army research, development, test, and evaluation was broken down as follows: $1,596.8 million from the fiscal year 1970 appropriation; $12 million brought forward from prior-year accounts; $23.3 million from OSD emergency funds; and $0.2 million transferred to the General Services Administration.

In the President's Budget for fiscal year 1971, $1,717.9 million was requested for research and development activities: $80.1 million for research; $232.7 million for exploratory development; $397.4 million for advance development; $140.7 million for engineering development; $300.3 million for management and support; and $566.7 million for operational systems development. As fiscal year 1970 ended, neither authorization nor appropriation bills had passed the Congress. A joint resolution authorized the continuance of the research and development program for fiscal year 1971.

Research Programs

In addition to funding problems, other considerations led to curtailment of some Army research programs.

In Section 203 of the 1970 Military Procurement Authorization Act (Public Law 91–121), the Congress supplied guidelines for expenditure of funds on research projects:

None of the funds authorized to be appropriated by this Act may be used to carry out any research project or study unless such project or study has a direct or apparent relationship to a specific military function or operation.

Although Army policy on research has generally conformed to this principle in the past, the inclusion of the provision in the new legislation prompted a review of the current research and development program. Employing a detailed interpretation of the regulation by the Office of the Secretary of Defense, the Army research and development community examined 4,000 projects and studies for compliance with Section 203. Of these, fourteen did not meet the requirement, less than 0.35 percent of the total. Because of the obvious benefits of continued research in the areas covered by the fourteen projects, the Army recommended that they be continued under the auspices of other federal agencies.

As a result of the President's decision to renounce biological warfare, a biological research program was developed to attain a defensive capability against biological warfare. In the chemical areas, research and development continued on offensive materials necessary to maintain a deterrent retaliatory capability. Defensive research and development continued on the detection and warning of chemical agent attacks, individual and collective protection, medical therapy, and decontamination materials and equipment.

Research facilities excess to the needs of the Army as a result of the President's decision were identified, and planning began for their disposal. Considerable interest in these facilities was evidenced by other government agencies that participated in the planning.

The work done in the life sciences yielded some especially encouraging results in the past fiscal year. Army researchers isolated in tissue culture an agent which may be a cause of viral hepatitis, and intensive studies to characterize this agent were in progress. Thirty-four thousand volunteers received inoculations with a new type of meningococcal vaccine that has reduced the incidence of infection caused by one type of meningococcus in a controlled study. The Walter Reed Army Institute of Research, in a co-operative project with the National Institute of Health's Division of Biological Standards and a number of university contractors, developed an attenuated strain of human measles discovered in a basic virological study.

An advance came in the control of influenza with the improvement of methods of producing influenza vaccine and assaying its potency. Since an epidemic can be halted by the swift production of immunizing agents, new techniques which the Army helped to develop are of particular benefit; they allow the production of vaccines more rapidly after the isolation of the individual strain of flu virus.

A new and highly effective vaccine against epidemic typhus was tested in epidemic conditions in Burundi with gratifying results. In a similar case, the Army provided immediate assistance to Guatamala and El Salvador upon the outbreak of an epidemic of Venezuelan equine encephalitis. The U.S. Army Medical Research Institute of Infectious Diseases had developed the vaccine for this disease, which is potentially dangerous to humans, during work on the defense against biological agents. The U.S. Agency for International Development delivered large amounts of the serum, which checked and eradicated the danger.

In other projects, taxonomists have described a new species of mosquito from Thailand that may carry dengue fever. One species of mosquito was completely eliminated on an island in the Gulf of Mexico off Florida by sterilizing the male. A subhuman primate was discovered which regulates its body heat by sweating, a valuable model for Army research into the mechanics of perspiration.

Malaria remains an obstacle in U.S. Army operations in tropical areas. Previously unknown strains of malaria parasites have appeared in recent years. Many are resistant to previously standard methods of prevention or treatment developed during World War II. Over 250,000 compounds have undergone examination in a concerted effort to control the disease. Programs of drug testing now include *Aotus* monkeys infected with drug-resistant strains of human malaria, as well as tests involving human malaria parasites in isolated blood cells.

The Army continued to search for new insect repellants that will stay on the skin longer, even under extreme conditions of heat and sweating. An improved chlorine test for the potability of drinking water also contributed to the protection of the combat soldier. The incidence of bacterial and fungal skin diseases in Vietnam led to the development of a new method for studying them, and for the first time, controlled human studies in the pathenogenesis and treatment of fungal infections are possible. The prophylactic use of griseofulvin has reduced the number of cases of skin infection of all kinds. Research into the causes of prickly heat revealed that it is a form of heat exhaustion due to a temporary malfunction in normal sweat glands. New media for culture development have improved the laboratory analyses of infections and have reduced their cost.

The Army has found that by adding adenine to stored blood, the shelf life of the blood is increased. This formula is now used in Southeast Asia.

The Army also investigated the adverse effect of smoking on operations at altitude. Tests documented a decrease in the ability of hemoglobin to transport oxygen to the tissues in man after smoking. Although this effect is already known, the Army remains interested in how smoking may impede the performance of mountain troops and aircraft pilots.

Dental research developed a new technique for a quickly applied splint for simple jaw fracture, which was used successfully in Vietnam and in the United States. The Army maintains a comprehensive program to apply decay-preventive fluoride to each soldier's teeth. Though a large proportion of men in the service receive this treatment from a dentist, most soldiers have been supplied with fluoride toothpastes in an effort to extend this protection to the whole service.

The analysis of food staples used by the Army determined that the eight sugar and sugar phosphate compounds found in such common vegetables as fresh carrots offer possibilities for the development of safe and natural additives to improve the taste of rations. Work on beef revealed that the aroma of the meat derives from certain intramuscular lipids. These studies and one on moisture and vapor in dehydrated experimental foods led to new packaging concepts for military rations and produced fresher tasting food with a longer shelf life.

Operational testing of a helicopter-borne crash rescue and fire fighting system which had been proposed as standard equipment revealed that the system could not be deployed rapidly enough after a crash to promote crew survival in fires that most often accompany helicopter mishaps. In a related area, the Army adopted a new helmet for air crewmen which is lighter, affords better sound attenuation than older models, employs an unbreakable sun visor, and has an improved suspension for better retention on impact.

Several new items of medical equipment were tested and developed. A dispenser which does not influence the flight characteristics of helicopters is now mounted without modification to the airframe to disperse insecticide dust and granules. Medical officers in the field are using a new wet bulb temperature kit to determine when conditions might cause heat casualties among trainees. The Special Forces have received a prototype portable surgical lamp designed to assist in bringing medical treatment to cases in remote areas. A dental hygienist set and a mobile X-ray stand are now standard equipment. A study has shown the feasibility of a lightweight automatic lens-fabricating machine that will produce new safety eyeglass lenses in the field, thus eliminating the delay encountered in having spectacles replaced at fixed rear area support bases.

In the field of animal husbandry, the Army organized a breeding experiment for the German Shepherd stock that has served so well as scout dogs in Vietnam. Studies identified the micro-organism which caused the hemorrhagic disease that killed 175 dogs in Southeast Asia, and researchers are now attempting to develop a vaccine.

Advanced Ballistic Missile Defense Program

The Advanced Ballistic Missile Defense Agency (ABMDA) of the Office, Chief of Research and Development, manages a program to continue the work begun under the Nike-X Advanced Development Program and the Advanced Research Project Agency's Project Defender, transferred to the Army after the decision to deploy the Sentinel (Safeguard) system. The ABMDA is responsible for advanced system and component development necessary to counter the Soviet threat to U.S. strategic offensive forces and their command and control centers; development of new system concepts and components which result in increased ballistic missile defense effectiveness; development of technology to counter a sophisticated threat to American cities from the Soviet Union or from Communist China; and the use of experimental facilities to assist in evaluating the effectiveness of American strategic offensive forces by the acquisition of data from re-entry and penetration tests employing U.S. missiles. To meet these requirements, the ABMDA pursues technology developments in radar systems, interceptor missiles, optics, data processing, target discrimination, re-entry physics, and nuclear effects.

The Army is now working on new systems concepts and components to defend the Minuteman system and to counter a postulated larger and more sophisticated Soviet force than the current U.S. Safeguard system can accommodate. This Hardsite defense system would supplement Safeguard with a larger number of defense modules, each defending a small portion of the Minuteman force. The radars of this system would be smaller, simpler, and cheaper than the Safeguard radars, and the system would be less costly than the proliferation of Safeguard components.

The Army has contributed to the research and development of high speed computers needed to assure that their data-handling capacity is adequate for the more severe threats.

Radar research has concentrated on the high-powered phased array radar with multibeam capability and a low susceptibility to countermeasures. Increased reliability and efficiency are being sought through the development of solid state radar components.

Advances have also been made in terminal interceptor technology areas offering accurate control under the stress of high speed and acceleration, in order to deal with highly maneuverable re-entry vehicles. Advanced studies continue on the feasibility of a long-range homing interceptor that destroys, through nuclear or nonnuclear means, re-entry vehicles in mid-course before they can endanger the United States.

Concurrently, effective schemes are being developed to discern a warhead from various penetration aids an attacker might use. This feat is accomplished by measurement and analysis of radar and optical data obtained during missile tests.

The Safeguard System Office and the ABMDA retain interrelated but separate research and development programs, the latter organization being charged with the development of components and technology to counter threats that will be beyond the capability of Safeguard. The work on more advanced systems is intended to provide options in the event that defense officials find themselves pressed to improve upon Safeguard in the face of new and increased threats from abroad.

Research and Development and Vietnamization

Until recently only limited channels existed through which the Army could determine the research and development requirements of the South Vietnamese. In December 1969, procedures were arranged between the Military Assistance Command, Vietnam (MACV), and the U.S. Army, Vietnam (USARV), command structure to permit the U.S. Army to extend research and development support to the South Vietnamese Army.

The USARV organization known as ACTIV (Army Concept Team in Vietnam) was designated as the nucleus of the research and development effort in Vietnam under the Vietnamization program, to handle those requirements for the Vietnamese Army while continuing to perform the combat developments and materiel evaluation mission in support of U.S. forces. ACTIV provides technical assistance to host country units and their advisers concerning hardware requirements. New equipment developed for U.S. use and potentially suitable for use by the Vietnamese Army is evaluated by units of both countries.

In March 1970, two channels were developed through which the Military Assistance Command may gather information on which to base decisions for Vietnamese Army requirements. The first channel centers on requests coming from U.S. advisers and South Vietnamese elements seeking answers to specific problems that would require new designs or modifications. Requests arising from these sources move through regular advisory channels to MACV headquarters. The second channel works in reverse, forwarding new equipment designed for the U.S. Army to South Vietnam for combat evaluation. These items are evaluated by ACTIV and the Vietnamese at their Combat Development Test Center; the results of the combined evaluations are forwarded to MACV headquarters and then through routine U.S. Army, Vietnam, and U.S. Army, Pacific, channels to the continental United States.

With these procedures, American and Vietnamese operational forces can readily determine their requirements, and the Vietnamese receive the same research and development support as the U.S. Army.

STANO Systems

The Army has given high priority to surveillance, target acquisition, and night observation devices and techniques. In November 1969, a separate division was established in the Office, Chief of Research and Development, to manage developments in this high priority field. The surveillance, target acquisition, and night observation (STANO) division manages programs in night vision, radar, special purpose detectors, and unattended ground sensors.

Two night vision devices have already been successful in operations in Vietnam. The first is a system mounted aboard a helicopter gunship which allows the pilot to search out targets at night and to engage them with his standard armaments. More of these units will be sent to Southeast Asia by the end of fiscal year 1971. A second night vision device is the hand-held infrared viewer. Designed primarily as a target acquisition device, the viewer has shown an unexpected ability to detect newly placed mines.

A laser target designation system has proved itself doubly valuable in solving the navigation problem in attempts to find small landing or drop zones during field operations. Landing zones now can be marked with laser beams on the ground, and supporting helicopters and troop lift ships identify the zone by laser-seekers mounted on the aircraft.

The Army is procuring test models of an eighteen-pound ground surveillance radar for use by forward troops. With miniaturized and integrated circuitry, the AN/PPS-15 is operated by one man and is well suited to small unit patrol action. For base defense, the Army is building a radar system capable of penetrating dense foliage and of scanning an entire perimeter. A new German- and French-developed long-range radar is being modified to replace the ten-year-old U.S. Army surveillance set, AN/TPS-25. Work continued on the mortar-locating radar, AN/TPQ-28, and a longer range counterbattery radar. Similar projects have defined specifications for artillery counterbattery radars.

Based on experience in Southeast Asia, the Army has studied the possibilities for worldwide use of unattended electronic sensors and is exploring alternatives for a system capable of worldwide deployment. The direction of this program will be more fully determined by the end of fiscal year 1971.

Firepower

In the area of conventional weapons, several of the Army's current programs underwent extensive review for the reduction of production costs or for contract defaults. In spite of some difficulties, the programs in new ordnance yielded data and engineering knowledge on which to base new developments in the future.

The joint effort with the Federal Republic of Germany, under which the main battle tank 70 (MBT–70) has been developed, was modified to a co-operative program in the middle of the fiscal year. Changes in the U.S. design were recommended to decrease production costs and increase the reliability of the vehicle; sacrifices in combat effectiveness were minimal. In December 1969, the new program was reviewed in the Office of the Secretary of Defense and in the following month the recommended changes were approved. The design changes have thus reduced the estimated unit cost of the tank by almost 30 percent. With the modification of the program and of the co-operative features of the engineering effort, the tank received a new designation, XM–803; the composite nomenclature MBT–70/XM–803 is to be used until February 1971.

The program to develop the novel AH–56A Cheyenne attack helicopter faltered amid contract difficulties in this fiscal year, but technical progress continued. The fire control and weapons subsystems met specification accuracy in aerial firing, and with an improved rotor control assembly, the vehicle demonstrated a true air speed of 186 knots. A night vision system for the aircraft was bench tested satisfactorily, and the aircraft weapons system was demonstrated for Defense Department officials during April 1970, when its complete design armament including the TOW missile was fired. The prime contractor, Lockheed Aircraft, appealed to the Secretary of Defense for relief after experiencing financial difficulties following the proceedings for contract default brought by the Army (see chapter 8; see also the 1969 annual report). As the fiscal year ended, the secretary was still considering these requests.

On November 4, 1969, the Senate and House Armed Services Committees Conference Report directed the Army to re-evaluate the Shillelagh and TOW missiles with an eye toward substituting the Shillelagh for the TOW in order to meet the Army's requirement for an antitank weapon for both the helicopter and infantry.

The re-evaluation for the infantry application, completed in March 1970, addressed the cost, schedules, and operational effectiveness of the two systems. The findings were that the substitution of Shillelagh for TOW would delay the fielding of an acceptable heavy antitank-assault weapon for at least four years, result in no dollar savings, be less satisfactory from an operational viewpoint, and introduce the inherent risk of any development program. (Shillelagh was designed to be fired from a closed breech in an armored vehicle; in infantry and helicopter roles, an open breech launcher and miniaturized guidance and control components would have to be developed and tested.) The Army therefore recommended to the Congress that the TOW program be continued and that no further consideration be given to Shillelagh as a basic heavy infantry weapon. As the fiscal year closed, the re-evaluation of the Shillelagh and TOW missiles as helicopter-borne armament remained under study.

The first tactical communications satellite has been in a synchronous orbit for over a year, and all the services continued to test its performance with a variety of super high frequency (SHF) and ultra high frequency (UHF) terminals of advanced design. The Army remained the lead service, procuring prototype tactical terminals from the prime contractor, Radio Corporation of America (RCA).

During the past fiscal year, the Army completed tests with ten UHF and eight SHF terminals. These terminals are constructed in five basic types: a one-man back pack for listening only that plays out printed alert or address messages; a three-man team pack which transmits and receives; a jeep-mounted version with an alert message receiver; a transceiver; and a teletype. A larger shelter-installed terminal can be transported by a 1¼-ton truck, a larger helicopter, or a cargo aircraft. As the year closed, the Army was testing a UHF terminal in a UH–1 helicopter.

X. Civil Works and Military Engineering

Army engineering efforts are divided into two major functional areas: public works and military engineering. As might be expected, some activities are common to both fields, even while they are applied in a civil environment on the one hand and a military environment on the other. As they are divergent in application, these activities are treated in a functional rather than a topical manner in this chapter.

Water Resources Development

As the primary developer and manager of the nation's water resources, the Department of the Army's Corp of Engineers is at the hub of one of the most critical issues facing the country today: how to serve the needs of an increasing population with a multitude of water uses without upsetting the cycles of nature that sustain all life.

Public Works and the Environment

During the last several years, increasing public concern for environmental quality has been reflected in a series of administrative changes aimed at adapting the Army Department's water resources program to meet changing public goals. Policy was established to consider environmental impact and to make projects as attractive as possible. Libby Dam, under construction on the Kootenai River in Montana, was designed with the aid of a landscape architect to fit the natural landscape and present a pleasing appearance. Planting trees and seedlings is a general practice at projects. Other beautification measures include using trees to screen hurricane barrier dikes in urban areas, landscaping soil banks along channels, aligning channels and floodways to preserve adjacent vegetation and scenery, and clearing reservoir pool areas to avoid unsightly exposure of dead trees.

To provide a broad range of environmental expertise, experience, and perspective, the Army's Chief of Engineers established a six-member environmental advisory board in April 1970. The board meets quarterly, provides advice on specific policies, programs, and problems, and contributes to an enhanced mutual understanding between the Corps of Engineers, the general public, and the conservation community.

The National Environmental Policy Act of 1969 requires that, with every project recommendation, information be provided on the environmental impact, any adverse environmental effects, alternatives to the proposed action, the relationship between man's local short-term uses of the environment and the maintenance and enhancement of long-term productivity, and any irreversible or irretrievable commitments of resources which would be involved. The possible alternatives, which include the status quo, and an economic, social, and environmental analysis for each are indicated.

The problem of water pollution has involved the Army's Corps of Engineers in a wide variety of water quality control activities, including abating waste disposal in navigable waterways, preventing and reducing pollution originating on Army-owned lands, providing treatment facilities for the corps' floating plant and reservoir recreation facilities, regulating streamflow for increased oxygenation and optimum water quality, developing acceptable measures for projects to comply with newly established federal and state water quality standards, and devising methods for disposal of polluted dredged material.

Sweeping new changes in Army regulations pertaining to issuing permits for work in navigable waters were announced in May 1970. The changes require that greater emphasis be given to environmental factors in evaluating permit applications, and reemphasize that the Corps of Engineers is concerned with the impact a proposed project may have not only on navigation but also on fish and wildlife, water quality, economics, conservation, aesthetics, recreation, water supply, flood damage prevention, and ecosystems in general.

Before issuing permits for dumping in navigable waters, the Army Corps of Engineers requires complete reports on waste content. The Water Quality Improvement Act of 1970 requires certification by the state or interstate agency responsible for water quality, or by the Secretary of the Interior, to the effect that there is reasonable assurance that the permitted activity will not violate water quality standards.

The corps can take legal action against polluters under the Refuse Act of 1899, which gives the Engineers authority to ban from navigable waters all wastes except domestic sewage. When industries are negligent or outside the law, the Army can recommend that the Department of Justice prosecute.

Construction and Management

Since 1936 the Army Corps of Engineers has completed over 669 flood control projects. Corps projects of all categories that contribute to effective flood control have prevented well over $18 billion in damages since 1918. In addition to many major reservoir projects, seventy-eight specifically authorized construction projects were under way during fiscal year 1970 to provide flood protection to local communities. Many small projects were also constructed under general authorities.

The federal program to improve rivers and harbors for navigation, now in its 144th year, was the first water resource development activity assigned to Army Engineers. The program consists of three major elements: coastal harbors and channels, Great Lakes harbors and channels, and inland and intracoastal waterways. Each of these systems has more than justified construction and operating costs by savings in transportation costs. For example, the federal government has improved in varying degrees some 22,000 miles of inland and intracoastal waterways, of which about 19,000 are currently in commercial use. Latest available statistics indicate that foreign and domestic traffic on inland waterways increased 3.4 percent during calendar year 1968 to establish a new record of 291.4 billion ton-miles.

In addition to providing flood control and aiding navigation, a great number of the corps' projects also generate pollution-free hydroelectric power. In fiscal year 1970, 1,156,500 kilowatts of generating capacity were placed in commercial operation. At the end of the fiscal year, a total of 12,031,900 kilowatts of generating capacity was in operation at fifty-three projects located in twenty states, representing 3.8 percent of the total generating capacity of the nation.

One public use of the water resource that has skyrocketed in recent years is that of recreation. In 1969, over 254 million visits to the corps' reservoirs were recorded, making the Army the conductor of the largest recreation program in the federal government. The attendance figure is particularly significant when compared with the sixteen million visits recorded in 1950. Large multiple-purpose reservoirs, such as the Walter F. George lock and dam on the Chatahoochee River bordering Alabama and Georgia and the Dworshak Reservoir now under construction on the North Fork of the Clearwater River in Idaho, provide excellent opportunity for camping, water sports, and related activities. Typical recreation facilities include tent and trailer sites, picnic areas, boat launching ramps, swimming beaches, and sanitary facilities, as well as visitor centers and overlooks. Many of the larger areas are leased to states and counties for public park and recreation use. Most of the remaining public use areas are operated by the corps.

The fiscal year 1970 appropriation for the Army Corps of Engineers water resources program was $1.145 billion, which covers investigations and surveys, planning, construction, and the operation and maintenance of flood control, river and harbor, beach protection, and hydroelectric projects.

Construction activities were performed on 266 specifically authorized navigation, flood control, and multiple purpose projects during the fiscal year. Construction on the $1.25 billion multiple-purpose plan for the Arkansas River and its tributaries in Arkansas and Oklahoma continued on schedule. Twelve of the seventeen locks and dams are in operation, and the navigation channel is now open from the Mississippi River to Fort Smith, Arkansas. The remaining five locks and dams are scheduled to be placed in operation by the end of 1970. In addition to opening a large portion of the land-locked interior of the Southwest to year-round water transportation, the project will provide flood control, produce hydroelectric power, permit low-flow regulation, and furnish opportunities for outdoor recreation.

Dworshak Reservoir, an important project in the Columbia River Basin, is 52 percent complete. Scheduled for storage in June 1972 and for power generation in November 1972, it will also provide flood control, navigation, and recreation benefits. The reservoir will have the highest concrete gravity dam in the United States, 723 feet high. The largest steelhead trout fish hatchery in the world has been constructed as a part of the project.

Another important multiple-purpose project in the Columbia River Basin is Libby Dam on the Kootenai River in Montana, which will provide benefits from flood control, power production, and recreation. Relocations necessitated by the project include 60 miles of railway and 118 miles of roads and highways. The over-all project is over 70 percent complete.

In Tennessee, the J. Percy Priest Reservoir located in the Cumberland River Basin is near completion. The combination earth and concrete gravity structure is 2,176 feet long and 147 feet high. The power plant, an integral part of the dam, will have a capacity of 33,000 kilowatts in a single unit. The project will provide flood control benefits in the metropolitan area of Nashville.

To think only of dams, dikes, and diversions in connection with flood problems is to overlook the important fact that a flood problem is related as much to the area subject to flooding—the flood plain—as it is to the flood. Over the years, efforts have been concentrated on controlling floods by structural means. Only recently has substantial attention been given to proper use of the flood plain as a means of limiting the susceptibility of the land to flood damage. Increasing recognition of environmental attributes of the flood plain—and of the larger area of which it is a part—is being given in corps survey investigations and reports. This broad approach is also presented as part of the planning assistance furnished to communities under the Flood Plain Management Services Program, which has produced nearly 400 flood plain information reports on about 1,000 locations throughout the nation, and has furnished flood hazard information on several thousand sites. Nearly 700 locales have used these reports in some phase of land use and related planning. About 185 have adopted or strengthened land use regulations—an important step forward in slowing the increase in the nation's flood losses.

Emergency Assistance

The major emergency activity engaged in by the Army Engineers in fiscal year 1970 was caused by Hurricane Camille, the most intense hurricane on record to enter the U.S. mainland. The toll was 128 deaths, 57 people missing, 17,914 homes destroyed or severely damaged, and $1.68 billion in damages in Mississippi and Louisiana. A broad band of rainfall caused by the hurricane resulted in flooding in Virginia, with $113 million in damages, 105 deaths, and 67 people missing.

In the stricken gulf coast area the Corps of Engineers engaged in disaster operations, closing breached levees and clearing navigation channels under statutory authorities. At the request of the corps, the Third Army ordered the 43d Engineer Battalion into the area to assist in recovery operations consisting mainly of clearing debris from roads and streets. Company D of the 818th Engineer Battalion and the 20th Construction Regiment (Navy) also assisted, all under the operational control of the Army's Mobile (Alabama) district engineer. At the request of the Office of Emergency Preparedness, the corps undertook a disaster assistance program under Public Laws 84–875 and 91–79 at a total estimated cost of $55 million. The corps also restored damaged flood control works and federally authorized shore protection structures and navigation facilities at an estimated cost of $12.3 million.

Planning

During the fiscal year the Army continued its activities as a member of the Federal Water Resources Council, with the Corps of Engineers participating directly in the activities of the Council of Representatives and the various supporting technical committees and work groups.

The Army continued its participation in the council's nationwide program of comprehensive river basin water resources development studies. The Corps of Engineers furnished members of the interagency co-ordinating committees and commissions established by the council to co-ordinate federal, state, and local planning for comprehensive river basin development. The river basin program consists of twenty framework studies and sixteen detailed type-2 studies; seven more of the latter are under consideration. One framework study has been completed and ten are in progress. Five type-2 studies have been completed by field-level co-ordinating committees. The reports submitted by the committees contain recommendations for water and related land resource development to meet the needs of both the near and distant future.

A necessity in careful resource planning is the involvement of the public in the planning process. To this end, a variety of communication techniques were tried in the Susquehanna Comprehensive River Basin Survey, nearing completion as the year closed. In addition, this study marked the first time in any federal water resources study that environmental quality was treated as one of the primary objectives for resource development and management. The plan will reflect, to the maximum degree feasible, publicly expressed preferences for environmental restoration and protection. The Federal Water Resources Council is considering adopting similar evaluation principles for water resources projects on a governmentwide basis.

As a result of the governmentwide planning, programing, and budgeting system (PPB), the Army Corps of Engineers has adopted a regional approach to multiyear investment planning. Nineteen program categories have been established for PPB purposes, consistent with regional boundaries defined by the Federal Water Resources Council. The regions are then broken down into river basins—131 basins in all. For each river basin, needs are then projected for urban flood damage reduction, rural flood damage reduction, water supply, commercial fisheries, recreation, navigation, and hydroelectric power.

The character and intensity of water resources problems and opportunities vary significantly among the major regions of the nation. Consequently, resource development needs and opportunities must be measured not only in physical terms but also in relation to the region's level of economic development and its concerns for environmental restoration or preservation.

During fiscal year 1970, primary attention was focused on refining estimates of need and on improving methods of program development to reveal more clearly the impact of alternative objectives. Through analysis of regional needs and objectives, a five-year water resources investment program, responsive to varying regional requirements, was submitted for consideration by the administration as a basis for selecting new construction and planning starts, and for allocating the funds available for civil works among the nineteen major national regions. Work continued on improving the PPB data base and in determining priorities for surveys to insure the timely response of civil works activities to emerging needs.

Research and Development

Research and development to support the civil works mission, funded at about $10.5 million in fiscal year 1970, continued to advance Corps of Engineers capabilities in conservation, utilization, and enhancement of the nation's inland and coastal water and related land resources.

Engineering research continued on soils, concrete, and other construction materials; on improvements in design techniques to assure more economical construction of locks and dams, with longer service life and lower operation and maintenance costs, and better able to resist earthquake forces; and on more efficient construction procedures. Continuing efforts were aimed at improving the analysis of hydrologic data, with special emphasis on water supply, water quality control, navigation improvement, and shore protection on the Great Lakes. The corps, as the designated U.S. lead agency for the joint U.S.-Canada International Field Year on the Great Lakes, a major component of the International Hydrological Decade, carried out the preparatory planning. Work continued on development of techniques for protecting coastal shores and beaches from erosive forces of waves and currents, and for minimizing shoaling of coastal harbors and channels. A start was also made on identifying the causes and establishing techniques for restoring or maintaining the usefulness and values of coastal inlets. Research was undertaken on developing practical methods for minimizing the annual losses resulting from ice jams on large northern rivers.

Fiscal year 1970 was the first full year of operation of the Institute for Water Resources. Activities of the institute principally concern research and study in three main areas: improving the scope, depth, and validity of economic evaluation; giving fuller consideration to social and environmental values and effects in the formulation of proposed water resources programs and projects; and improving the total planning process.

Research on preservation, enhancement, and utilization of environment received increased emphasis. Work continued on improving the assessment of water-oriented recreation demands, on determining the effects on biota of variations in reservoir releases and impoundments, and on formulating aesthetic criteria in the planning of water resource developments. Preliminary studies were made in identifying the effects of dredging, construction, and related developmental activities on ecological balance and environmental values.

Nuclear explosives appear to hold great promise for moving massive quantities of earth and rock economically. The knowledge of channel cutting and harbor construction by explosive means was advanced with the successful completion of a chemical explosives experiment, Project Pre-Gondola III, Phase III, by the U.S. Army Engineer Nuclear Cratering Group during the second quarter of the fiscal year. A channel between the reservoir at Fort Peck, Montana, and an existing row crater was cut on October 6, 1969, with the simultaneous detonation of five charges of aluminized ammonium nitrate slurry totaling seventy tons. The resulting navigable channel varies in width from 135 to 200 feet at water level and is about 35 feet deep.

Another experiment using chemical explosives was carried out at Kawaihae Bay, Hawaii, where a small boat harbor entrance channel and berthing basin was excavated in a series of detonations during the period from April 23 to May 8, 1970. Although the experiment demonstrated the value of chemical explosive excavation in creating a harbor, all charges did not detonate properly, and a small amount of remedial excavation work still remains to be done.

As a result of guidance by the Bureau of the Budget, the Nuclear Cratering Group will become a subordinate agency of the Waterways Experiment Station, the Corps of Engineers' largest research and development laboratory. The Nuclear Cratering Group will remain located at the Atomic Energy Commission's Lawrence Radiation Laboratory in Livermore, California, where it will emphasize its chemical explosive excavation program.

Military Activities and the Environment

The enactment of the National Environmental Policy Act of 1969 brought into focus the increasing national concern for the quality of the general environment and gave impetus to a variety of programs, in the military as well as the civil area, designed to protect both air and water from pollution. By Executive Order 11507 of February 5, 1970, President Nixon directed that the federal government would provide leadership in the nationwide effort to protect and improve the quality of the atmosphere and of water resources. Attention was to be given to these matters in the design, operation, and maintenance of federal facilities—buildings, installations, structures, public works, equipment, aircraft, vessels, and other vehicles and property owned by the government or constructed or manufactured for lease to the government.

As a result of prior programing, the Army in fiscal year 1970 funded $19 million for air and water pollution projects in the military construction, procurement, and operation and maintenance sections of the budget. About $40 million and $85 million respectively will be requested for these purposes in the budgets for fiscal years 1971 and 1972.

In fiscal year 1970, $100,000 was also allocated to develop policy and plans and begin operation of a program of limited research and testing of fuels, additives, and emission devices. Funding requests will be enlarged to a total of about $9.6 million for the five coming years. Investigations will cover equipment powered by gasoline, diesel, and turbine engines and their fuels. The Army has co-ordinated its efforts with those of other federal agencies, and especially with the Department of Health, Education, and Welfare. Army plans and programs are compatible with those developed by the National Air Pollution Control Administration. An Army representative will sit as a member of an advisory committee on advanced power systems that is assisting the Council on Environmental Quality.

In addition to the close attention paid by the Army to the preservation of the natural environment through the water resources development program described above, planning for the proper use of natural resources on Army installations was emphasized. Land, forest, and wildlife management plans include the development of recreation projects, the preservation of wildlife, and retention or restoration of natural beauty with landscape plantings and other vegetative cover. The Army-wide conservation program is applied over approximately thirteen million acres, of which 335,000 are improved grounds—areas that receive intensive turf grass management for dust and erosion control to provide lawns for buildup areas and turf for drill fields, aircraft landing fields, and athletic facilities. Also in the past year, improvements were made in the technical direction given to the forest management program, and active fish and wildlife programs were operated at 110 Army installations under co-operative plans with the Department of the Interior and state fish and game agencies.

National attention to air and water pollution control was reflected in activities related to existing Army facilities. Congress appropriated $6.4 million for construction of air pollution control projects and $6.6 million for construction of water pollution control projects. Further progress was also made in actions to eliminate open burning of refuse, procure fuels with lower sulfur content, and replace coal-fired heating plants with gas or oil units. Corrective actions for presently known sources of pollution will cost about $160 million.

Military Engineering Research and Development

Research in military engineering methods and techniques for support of the Army in the field was broadened and increased during the past year. As indicated previously, new designs for aircraft revetments were developed and disseminated to engineer units in the field. Development of shelters providing overhead cover was also initiated. A thin-walled metal arch structure having a clear span opening of eighty feet is a pilot item in the program. This structure is designed to support a two-foot-thick layer of concrete on top of the shell, which will provide protection from direct hits of most artillery, mortar, or rocket projectiles. The structure is large enough to shelter any Army aircraft.

Research has also continued on development of methods of locating covered sources of aggregates (gravels) in delta areas through analysis of various types of aerial photography. Excellent progress has been made to date in special construction materials maps which are being used to aid the LOC highway program in Vietnam.

In conjunction with the Air Force and Federal Aviation Administration, the Army Chief of Engineers is developing permanent design and evaluation criteria applicable to the Air Force C–5A and other multiwheeled and very heavy aircraft. Development of criteria for expedient pavement-surfacing of airfields for such aircraft in theaters of operations was also initiated. Initial test reports indicate present design theories and practices are adequate for portland cement concrete pavements and slightly conservative for asphaltic concrete pavements.

At the request of the U.S. Army, Vietnam, Engineer, a study was conducted to determine critical standoff distances for various types of bridge piers with regard to a variety of explosive charges. This study has led to the initiation of new research to develop the methodology for blowing the deck off a bridge by means of a water column produced by an explosion. Methods of protecting against this form of bridge demolition are also being investigated.

A pre-engineered collapsible and reusable battle area bunker system which can be emplaced by a squad of men in under eight hours was being developed. The system can be put into position without the use of special tools.

Investigation of a new method of constructing a roadbed without the use of gravel was initiated in fiscal year 1969 and is scheduled for completion in fiscal year 1971. The technique consists of encapsulating common soil in a durable, trafficable, watertight membrane. One of the primary features in the system is the ability to construct the roadbed over soft soils. Research presently indicates that a twelve-inch layer of the encased material, including the wearing surface, can be emplaced at a rate of approximately 300 feet an hour.

Research and testing was also continued in nuclear construction engineering under the Corps of Engineers portion of the Army's Nuclear Weapons Effects Research and Test program. Reports and technical papers on nuclear cratering, and on underground and underwater effects of nuclear weapons, were published. Data contained in these reports will be useful in design and construction of ballistic missiles and related defensive systems. A five-year, long-range, nuclear weapons effects research plan, which integrates the nuclear effects research required by numerous U.S. agencies, was developed and published by the Army.

Improvement and modernization of Army bridging capabilities continued. A cable-reinforcing kit for standard Bailey panel bridges was developed. This kit will increase allowable bridge loads by prestressing the Bailey bridge components. Development and testing for a mobile amphibious bridge-ferry (MAB) was completed. The bridge has been adopted and is being procured for troop use in Europe. The MAB consists of self-propelled amphibious transporters with bridge roadway superstructures which can be easily linked together to form a continuous bridge or rafts of various sizes and load capabilities. The mobility of these units and their speed of assembly will permit rapid assault crossings in support of military operations.

Development of a rapidly erectable floating bridge known as the ribbon bridge has proceeded. This bridge is designed to be erected in one-fifth the time of current comparable U.S. float bridging. Delivery of prototypes for testing is scheduled for December 1970. Two of the recently developed British medium girder fixed bridges are also being procured for confirmatory testing. These bridges, scheduled for delivery in mid-fiscal 1971, are made of high strength aluminum alloy components that can be assembled and installed rapidly, without heavy erection equipment, to support class-60 loads on spans up to 100 feet.

A new organizational concept for real property maintenance activities (RPMA) support in oversea theaters of operation was developed as a result of recommendations made by the Lincoln Board. The concept emphasized centralization and stovepiping of RPMA units in order to provide the technical supervision, coordination, and control by the theater Army staff engineer to insure more efficient use of available RPMA resources. Adoption of the concept will require the transfer of RPMA responsibility from theater Army service support elements to the theater Army engineer command; development of three new Army engineer organizations to provide an adequate organization capability for RPMA support; and modernization of the current service team series for augmentation of basic engineer units including the three new organizations. These new organizations, the facilities engineering team, group, and district, will serve as the framework upon which RPMA support is formed, and will be assigned to the Engineer command.

The facilities engineering team will serve as the basic mobile element for initial and immediate RPMA support for division-size forces in a theater of operations. It will deploy with a division-size force with equipment and any specialized tools needed to erect, operate, and maintain new or unique facilities. The team structure will contain a maximum number of operating craftsmen and a minimum essential amount of supervisory, management, and planning personnel.

The team will normally be replaced by the phased deployment of a facilities engineering group. The group will have a complete staff to plan, program, schedule, and account for the complete range of facilities engineering activities of the installation or area concerned, and a full complement of operating craftsmen to execute RPMA tasks.

In a large theater of operations, a facilities engineering district will provide the intermediate level of command, management, and administration necessary to control two to four facilities engineering groups. It will have only those technical craftsmen necessary for the proper planning, supervision, inspection, and accounting of RPMA tasks. Modern, sophisticated management systems will be employed to insure full utilization of RPMA resources, immediate response to emergencies, accounting for real property and funds, and long-range requirements planning and budget, materiel, and manpower programing.

Mapping and Geodesy

The U.S. Army Topographic Command (USATOPOCOM) completed three major projects which yielded large quantities of data for the precise determination of distances and directions, and determination of specific locations on the surface of the earth. Two of these programs, sequential collation of ranges (SECOR) and ballistic camera #4 (BC–4) employed satellites which were tracked electronically (SECOR) and optically (BC–4). The third program, designated as twelfth parallel survey, employed optical and electronic surveying instruments operated by ground survey parties. Observations from these projects are processed by computer and integrated into the topographic data bank. These data are used to increase man's knowledge of the size and shape of the earth, produce more accurate maps, and support national environmental and space programs. An associated program for measuring the variance of gravity of the earth's surface continued, and a follow-on program using the Doppler system for tracking electronic satellites was initiated to reinforce and refine previously accumulated topographic data.

USATOPOCOM also closed out operations of the 64th Engineer Battalion on the continents of Asia and Africa. Among the accomplishments of the battalion were completion of a 1200-mile-long arc of first-order triangulation in Libya, which closed the loop of geodetic survey around the Mediterranean Sea; establishment of survey control (latitude, longitude, and elevation) for approximately 1,250,000 square miles in Libya, Iran, Ethiopia, and Liberia as the first step in the new mapping of these countries; and collection of essential information concerning names of towns, rivers, and mountains, locations of boundaries, types of roads and bridges, and like data for approximately 1,000,000 square miles in these countries.

A third-generation computer (UNIVAC–1108) was delivered to the USATOPOCOM in June 1970. When acceptance tests are completed this computer will provide increased data processing capability; less efficient equipment will be phased out and costly contracts for computer support will be discontinued.

During fiscal year 1970 USATOPOCOM began to support the Army's new surveillance, target acquisition, and night observation (STANO) program and the field phase of that program, Project MASSTER. Topographic support is divided into two categories. The first involves the provision of topographic products and services necessary to carry out the STANO tests. The second is the development of techniques to determine soil conditions for effective location and emplacement of unattended ground sensors. Support is also being provided for the 524th Engineer Topographic Company (Corps) at Fort Hood, Texas, for the survey of test areas and the development of the unit's photogrammetric capabilities.

The U.S. Army Topographic Command has active co-operative agreements with the mapping agencies of more than fifty countries. In conjunction with these agencies the command has continued to provide a wide variety of topographic products to U.S. and Free World forces. It has also furnished assistance in the form of maps and topographic information to civilian agencies engaged in disaster relief operations, such as those following Hurricane Camille. The command also participated in the settlement of the Chile-Argentina boundary dispute by providing aerial photography, maps, and technical consultant services to the boundary commission.

XI. Special Functions

The Army is executive agent for the nation in several special functions in the fields of international and civil affairs, in addition to the civil defense and public works responsibilities covered in other chapters of this report. Among them are administration of the Ryukyu Islands, administration of the Panama Canal, sea level canal affairs, and supervision of a national program for rifle practice.

Administration of the Ryukyu Islands

The United States continued to administer the Ryukyu Islands under the provisions of Article 3 of the Treaty of Peace with Japan. The islands include Okinawa, where the U.S. maintains a large military base. The administration of the Ryukyus has been assigned by the President to the Secretary of Defense, who has delegated this responsibility to the Department of the Army. The field responsibility for governing this area is vested in the U.S. Civil Administration of the Ryukyu Islands (USCAR), headed by a high commissioner, who is appointed by the Secretary of Defense with the concurrence of the Secretary of State and the President's approval. An indigenous government exercises broad legislative, executive, and judicial authority in performing day-to-day governmental functions under the leadership of a popularly elected chief executive.

A historic meeting at Washington between President Nixon and Prime Minister Eisaku Sato of Japan during November 19–21, 1969, culminated in a decision to begin immediate negotiations for the reversion of the Ryukyus to Japan in 1972, after almost three decades of postwar separation. This planned territorial adjustment, which has few precedents in world history, will effectively fulfill the long-standing U.S. promise to return to Japan all of the islands acquired by Article 3 of the 1952 peace treaty. The other islands acquired thereby have already been returned.

The joint communiqué issued on November 21, 1969, to announce this co-operative decision stated that the U.S.-Japan Treaty of Mutual Cooperation and Security would be continued and would be extended to the Ryukyus without modification when reversion takes place. The United States would thus continue to maintain its military base on Okinawa for the mutual security of both countries and to help the United States fulfill its treaty commitments in the Far East.

To pave the way to reversion, the President and Prime Minister also agreed that the two governments would consult closely and co-operate on measures to ensure a smooth transfer of administrative rights, and that the U.S.-Japan Consultative Committee at Tokyo would undertake over-all responsibility for this preparatory work. They further decided to establish at Naha a preparatory commission (which was inaugurated on March 24, 1970) to consult and co-ordinate locally on reversion arrangements, including necessary assistance to the local government. The High Commissioner represents the United States on this commission, while Japan has a representative with ambassadorial rank; the Ryukyuan Chief Executive assists it in an advisory capacity. The formal reversion negotiations at Tokyo were initiated in April to prepare the detailed agreement covering the return of administrative rights.

To give Ryukyuans an opportunity to participate in Japanese national affairs even before reversion, the United States and Japan worked out an agreement whereby elected Ryukyuan representatives would be permitted to sit in the Japanese Diet—five in the House of Representatives and two in the House of Councillors. Japanese legislation to this effect was passed early in 1970, and Ryukyuan legislation on the related electoral arrangements was being readied for enactment as the period ended.

Despite the fact that the Ryukyuan economy is heavily dependent upon the large U.S. military base on Okinawa and that a great number of Ryukyuan workers depend upon it for their livelihood, the Ryukyuan people are perennially sensitive to certain military activities around them. However, local feelings on these issues were somewhat quieted by the Nixon-Sato reversion understanding. Furthermore, Ryukyuan concern about the recurring visits of nuclear submarines was largely allayed by the co-ordinated public-safety efforts of American and Ryukyuan authorities in various sophisticated radioactivity-monitoring programs. Deep Ryukyuan concern about the storage of chemical munitions on Okinawa was tempered by U.S. assurance that these munitions would be removed from Okinawa at an early date.

There was a notable expansion of commercial air travel to the Ryukyus, reflecting an increased appreciation on the part of tourists and commercial travelers for Okinawa's key location in the crowded western Pacific air corridors. Trans World Airlines added an Okinawa stop to its worldwide service for the first time, and Flying Tiger considerably expanded its existing service. Okinawa is now served by eight airlines, one of which provides interisland service. The volume of air passengers passing through the Civil Air Terminal at Naha increased from 186,662 in 1965 to 583,948 by the end of 1969. To accommodate this burgeoning activity, steps were initiated to expand the commercial facilities at the Naha Civil Air Terminal. Specifically, design and construction of new facilities, costing an estimated $25 million, was undertaken by the U.S. government in collaboration with the government of Japan, which will defray almost all of the cost. The new facilities will include additional aircraft loading and maneuver areas, a new terminal building with 21,000 square meters of floor space, extensive parking facilities, and the usual accessories of modern air passenger traffic. Travel-control procedures were streamlined during the period as a means of facilitating travel between the Ryukyus and Japan. Most of the approximately 300,000 persons who visited the Ryukyus during the year came from Japan.

U.S. financial expenditures in and contributions to the Ryukyu Islands, which reached the level of $288 million during this period (as compared to $271 million in fiscal year 1969), not only contributed substantially to Okinawa's economic development but also helped to offset much of its import-export gap. Of the U.S. input $34.6 million was in the form of outright grants—$17.5 million directly appropriated by Congress and $17.1 million allocated from the proceeds of various business activities of the U.S. Civil Administration. The latter included the purchase and resale of petroleum products, the operations of certain public utility corporations (such as the Ryukyu Electric Power Corporation and the Ryukyu Domestic Water Corporation), and investment loans by the Bank of the Ryukyus. These extensive grants financed important programs in the fields of education, electric power, highway, construction, sewage disposal, public health, technical training, water supply, public safety, and public housing.

Budgetary constraints of the worldwide U.S. economy program necessitated sizable manpower reductions in the Ryukyuan work force of the U.S. forces, and these cuts predictably evoked widespread protests, including several brief strikes and work stoppages. However, employee resentment on this score was notably reduced toward the end of the period due to the satisfactory conclusion of certain collective bargaining arrangements between the Joint Services Labor Committee of the U.S. forces and the union representatives of their Ryukyuan employees.

U.S. programs for developing Ryukyuan human resources continued to receive special attention. Some $1 million was allocated specifically for the advanced education and training of about 300 Ryukyuan exchange visitors in the United States, including graduate and undergraduate students, national leaders, technical trainees, and faculty members of the University of the Ryukyus. In the field of community relations, the Ryukyuan-American People-to-People Program was popular and highly successful. The major part of such activities was carried out co-operatively by personnel of the U.S. forces and Ryukyuan groups in the several communities. Such activities filled genuine local needs by improving school facilities, recreational opportunities, village roads, and water supplies; by promoting measures to further public health and sanitation; and by making volunteer American instructors available to provide English language training.

Administration of the Panama Canal

By authority delegated to him as the personal representative of the President, the Secretary of the Army has special responsibilities for Panama Canal matters, which include operations of the Canal Zone government and Panama Canal Company. The Canal Zone government is administered under the supervision of the Secretary of the Army by the governor of the Canal Zone, who is appointed by the President. Management of the Panama Canal Company is vested in a board of directors appointed by the Secretary of the Army as "stockholder," representing the interest of the United States as owner of the corporation. The Secretary of the Army has appointed the Under Secretary of the Army as a member and Chairman of the Board.

In fiscal year 1970, 14,829 oceangoing ships, including 1,068 U.S. government vessels, passed through the canal. Toll revenues were approximately $100.9 million, which included credits for transits of U.S. government vessels. Panama Canal revenues are applied against operating and capital expenses of the canal enterprise. Detailed financial statements are published in the annual reports of the Panama Canal Company and Canal Zone government. The toll figure for 1970 represented an increase of almost $5 million over 1969.

Interoceanic Canal Studies

Determining the feasibility of building a new sea-level canal to accommodate the increasing number and size of ships desiring to use such a waterway is the task of the Atlantic-Pacific Interoceanic Canal Study Commission. The commission report is scheduled to be forwarded to the President on December 1, 1970. The Department of the Army represents the Department of Defense on this presidential commission, with the Chief of Engineers acting as the engineering agent for the commission and directing the engineering feasibility portion of the study.

Field studies, in conjunction with available information, provided the basis for engineering judgment on the alternatives of constructing an interoceanic sea-level canal or modernizing the existing lock canal. Field operations were terminated in July 1969, but data evaluation continued until June 1970. The engineering feasibility study was to be presented to the study commission in August 1970. The entire report was scheduled to be forwarded to the President on December 1, 1970.

As the year closed, a group chaired by the Deputy Under Secretary of the Army (IA) was studying the defense aspects of an interoceanic sea-level canal, its report to be presented to the canal study commission in August 1970.

From an engineering point of view, all the routes considered for conventional excavation are feasible. The preferred one is Route 10, about ten miles southwest of and parallel to the present canal. Second is Route 14, which closely follows the Panama Canal alinement. These routes would cost about $3 billion and take about thirteen years to construct. Other routes are far more costly.

The feasibility of nuclear excavation has not been established because the inability to conduct nuclear cratering tests up into the megaton range has left too many uncertainties. The timetable for conducting such tests cannot be predicted. If nuclear excavation were feasible and could be accomplished as its proponents believe, Route 25 in northwestern Colombia, which is estimated at slightly over $2 billion, might be the preferred route. Most of this expense is for the conventionally excavated section of the route. All-nuclear routes investigated are not considered possible because of safety costs or unsuitable geologic conditions.

Promotion of Rifle Practice

During fiscal year 1970, the reorientation of the Civilian Marksmanship Program toward the support of junior shooters was almost completed. As the year closed, support was being provided to junior shooters between the ages of twelve and nineteen whose period of service participation lies ahead of them.

The number of clubs supported by the Office of the Director of Civilian Marksmanship (ODCM) during fiscal year 1970 steadily decreased because of the requirements for clubs to support junior shooters. About 3,100 clubs with an individual membership of 220,000 are affiliated with and receive support from the ODCM.

During fiscal year 1970, the National Board for the Promotion of Rifle Practice (NBPRP) sponsored forty-two regional excellence-in-competition matches where civilian and military personnel competed to earn credits toward award of the Distinguished Rifleman or Distinguished Pistol Shot badge. During the year, approximately seventy-five excellence in competition badges and thirty-seven distinguished badges were awarded to civilian participants. Individual services of the armed forces award these badges under rules and regulations administered by the NBPRP.

Army support for the 1970 National Matches, as in 1968 and 1969, has not been granted because of budget austerity and the commitment in Southeast Asia. The decision to support these matches will continue to be made on a yearly basis. Three hundred National Match .30-caliber M1 rifles were authorized for sale to competitive high power rifle shooters in April 1970. These sales will result in a return of $46,000 to the United States Treasury.

XII. Summary

The reader of the foregoing will have found a definite theme in Army operations in fiscal year 1970, one that took its lead from national trends. Whether the subject is funds, personnel, strength, training, combat, casualties, construction, research, development, procurement, or production, the tendency was toward reduction. Curtailment, consolidation, withdrawal, retrenchment, adjustment, constraint—these are the watchwords that set the tone of Army operation in 1970 and charted the directions for the coming year.

The general downward turn in personnel and fund levels, with little change in functions, placed a premium on the management of resources, and a widespread effort was in progress during the year to streamline all facets of operation and make the most economical and effective use possible of money and manpower.

Several important developments in the Vietnam War are noted in the report. On the battlefield, the operations against enemy sanctuaries in Cambodia were patently significant, ousting the Viet Cong and North Vietnamese from previously secure areas and causing them to lose sizable stocks of supplies and operational initiatives planned for the Mekong Delta region. At the same time, the South Vietnamese forces that participated in the strikes acquired valuable operational experience.

Details of the Vietnamization program, under which the United States seeks to qualify the host country to assume the primary burden of its own defense, emerge through this report. It is a measure of the progress of allied battlefield operations and the Vietnamization program that 115,000 American troops, over half of them Army, were withdrawn during the year, while plans were projected for further substantial reductions in fiscal year 1971.

Several cases involving alleged battlefield misconduct drew national attention and a broad Army investigative effort during the year, inspiring a comprehensive review and a variety of actions relating to policies, procedures, and training in this general field.

The President's action in renouncing American use of lethal biological agents and weapons as well as chemical toxins and the first use of lethal chemical and incapacitating chemical agents was a milestone in military affairs and an active initiative for peace.

The broad lines of adjustment to a postwar posture are evident in numerous actions outlined in various functional sections of the report. Extending from the battlefront back through the theater and the continental base and up to the departmental headquarters, these actions are designed to promote economy, avoid waste, insure maximum use of materiel through redistribution, make optimum use of personnel skills, preserve unit readiness, refine structure and organization, and in general maintain a force capable of carrying out the Army's role in national defense. These are, indeed, the principles and practices that guide the Army as it moves into a new fiscal year.

Index

www.ingramcontent.com/pod-product-compliance
Lightning Source LLC
Chambersburg PA
CBHW031301090426
42742CB00007B/554